Eleven Wisconsin Poets:

A Whitewater Poetry Sampler

Edited with an Introduction by

DeWitt Clinton
The University of Wisconsin–Whitewater

K H

Kendall/Hunt
Publishing Company
Dubuque, Iowa

Cover photo courtesy of the Wisconsin Division of Tourism

Photographs by John Ziemann

Photograph of Ray Griffith by Greg Theune

Contents

Introduction

On any given day during the school year, you can walk by Art Madson's office and read one of his new poems, posted on his office door. If you do this often enough, poetry can become a part of your life, much as it has for a number of English department members. I always look forward to a new poem of Art's, and enjoy his enthusiasm for sharing new work with friends. I see him often visiting with a department colleague--hearing, listening, reacting to suggestions about his poetry.

It's that spirit of poets sharing poems with colleagues which prompted me to gather together a collection of poetry by the active, publishing poets of our department. And when three new poets joined our faculty in the fall of 1985, I realized we had a unique situation here in Whitewater, where a number of poets, all writing in different directions, all with different sensibilities of craft and material, had created, by serendipity, a special time for poetry. That is worth celebrating.

In the fall we organized a university-wide writer's workshop where creative writers from all colleges and departments were encouraged to share their work with others. During the spring, members of Friends of Poetry, a community-wide poetry workshop, invited those new faculty members to highlight the annual May Poetry Festival. So it was a year of seeing work by new poets, sharing and listening to different poetic principles, and realizing that here at Whitewater, a diverse group of poets had created a supportive poetry community.

Toward the end of the school year, with this feeling of celebration, I invited a number of the department poets, as well as a few from other departments, to contribute poems for an anthology which would represent each poet's "new and selected poems." I suggested that each contribution could be designed as a small collection for each author.

But there are other reasons for editing this anthology. For a number of years I have been using a variety of poetry textbooks for freshman composition classes. With each anthology, I always found more poetry which I didn't want to teach than poetry I was enthusiastic about. As something of an experiment,

I decided to take the best contemporary poems from those anthologies, and include one of mine, and present to my classes what I thought represented the best of contemporary poetry. Well the idea worked, or at least I thought so. I began to wonder, if this practice of using our university poets might interest more English 102 students. So I continued with the experiment, and you are now seeing the final result--an anthology of eleven University of Wisconsin--Whitewater poets--which can serve as a guide to at least a few of the directions and sensibilities of contemporary American poetry.

You will see a number of poems reflective of botany and wildlife; you will see even more poems reflective of human relationships; a few poets will take you to the jungles of Vietnam and Central America; one even takes you back to the WWII Dresden bombing. One poet has translated a few of his poems into German. One poet offers a brilliant insight into the horror of a nuclear holocaust on the route from Whitewater to Madison, another offers the celebration of a new body.

Another sings praises of human sexuality, and another takes us back to the Civil War. One poet has taken great delight with making list poems and another explores the dark, Dracula side of human nature. Wisconsin landscape is celebrated in a number of poems, and one poet takes us back to the age of dinosaurs. Folklore and charms, Christmas pasts, Nicaragua, philosophical questions, Canadian fishing holes, Snow White, county fairs, childhood memories, descriptions from Punjab, India, solar flares and the powers of animals, head hunting and baleen whales--all of these are explored, and much more, in poetic forms which are accessible to not only university students, but to anyone interested in poetry that offers insight into our human condition.

Poetry, at least as I teach it in my classes of English 102, is an introspective art which calls for a special relationship between poet and reader. With each poet, take your time to become acquainted with the author's work. Each poem was probably written several times, through several drafts, and possibly will change even a few more times. The study questions at the end of each poet's selections should help you sort out both your feelings and your insights into these poets. But if you still have questions, look the poet up as this is the unique part of the anthology--that you can read poems by our faculty, have the opportunity to visit with them in the hallways or their offices and learn, on a much more personal level, what poetry is and how it affects our lives.

Introductions say everything and nothing. They are designed to raise your curiosity about the book in your hands. We've waited long enough, talked enough about it, and now, it's time to explore and read these poets.

DeWitt Clinton
Whitewater, Wisconsin
September 15, 1986

Acknowledgments

DeWitt Clinton

"Night Jungle Bird Life" appeared in *Strange Fruit,* 1983, and reprinted in *Night Jungle Bird Life,* 02 Press, 1983; "Bullet" appeared in *Night Jungle Bird Life;* "Feeling Oddly Cold Then Wingéd as a Bat" and "The Birds Do Chirp Thy Still and Very Heart" appeared in *Active Death: Unholy Rhymes,* Count Dracula Fan Club, 1986; "Sniper to Point" appeared in *Deros,* Spring, 1986.

Gay Davidson

"Crossing the Newville Bridge" appeared in *Windfall,* 1985; "Drumlin" appeared in *Wisconsin Poets Calendar,* 1982, and reprinted in the *Publication for the Study of Midwestern Literature,* Summer, 1986; "Head Hunting" appeared in the *Publication for the Study of Midwestern Literature,* Summer, 1986; "Swimming with My Mouth" appeared in a card series, Sackbut Press, Fall, 1984; "Slowpitch: Running Mantra #1" appeared in *Towers Magazine,* Fall, 1979.

Ron Ellis

"Scenes of Green Light" appeared in *Friends of Poetry,* Summer, 1979; "The Power of the Doe" appeared in *The Pikestaff Forum,* Spring, 1978, and reprinted in *Border Crossings: Minnesota Voices Project Reader,* New Rivers Press, 1984; "Addition" appeared in *Monmouth Review,* 1972, and reprinted in *Border Crossings;* "Raccoon" appeared in *The Hika Bay Review,* Summer, 1979; "Preserves" appeared in *New Jersey Poetry Journal,* Winter, 1983; "Spin-Off" appeared in *Poets On,* Winter, 1984.

Ray Griffith

"Roses" appeared in *Windfall,* Spring, 1986; "Rooms" appeared in *Light Year '86,* Bits Press, 1985; "Dewey Decimal" and "Ferns" appeared in *Light Year '85;* "Khajuraho" appeared in *Friends of Poetry,* 1981; "Songh" and "Balloon-Sellers" appeared in *Friends of Poetry,* 1980; "The Peacocks of Narangwal" appeared in *Agalumnus,* 1973.

Arthur Madson

"Cousins" appeared in *Ptolemy,* No. 9 & 10, 1983; "Boojum Tree" appeared in *Windfall,* No. 5, 1983; "She Hawk" and "Dinosaurs" appeared in *Because It's Sprung an Ooze,* 1982; "Height Report" appeared in *Mill Hunk Herald,* Fall, 1986; "Basic Training" appeared in *Find My Pelvis,* 1982.

Andrea Musher

"In Botswana" appeared in *Woman's Quarterly Review;* "On the Edge of the Desert" and "An Apocryphal Interview" appeared in *Madison Review;* "My Family" appeared in *On the Street;* "In Black Earth, Wisconsin" appeared in *Abraxas.*

Angela Peckenpaugh

"From a Letter by My Great Grandfather, Ham Chamberlayne, Virginian, at the Civil War Front, 1862, to Sally Grattan" appeared in *Virginia Quarterly Review,* 1977, and reprinted in *Letters from Lee's Army,* Morgan Press, 1979; "Gyromancy" appeared in *Wisconsin Academy Review,* June, 1982; "Charm of Disguise" appeared in *Wisconsin Academy Review* and reprinted in *A Book of Charms,* Barnwood Press, 1983; "To Capture the Power of a Day Lily," "Amaryllis," "Charm of a Child," and "Charm to Win at Poker" appeared in *A Book of Charms,* Barnwood Press, 1983; "The Bridge That Leads to Blue," appeared in *Discovering the Mandala,* Lakes and Prairies Press, 1981, and reprinted in *Gathering Place of the Waters;* "Rose" appeared in *Salthouse,* 1983; "Valentines" appeared in *John O'Hara Journal,* 1981; "Revival Meeting" won third prize, 1986 contest, Wisconsin Fellowship of Poets.

Dale Ritterbusch

"Search and Destroy" appeared in *Carrying the Darkness*, Avon, 1985.

Dennis Trudell

"The Art of Poetry" appeared in *Quickly Aging Here*, Doubleday; "Central American Village" appeared in *Prairie Schooner;* "A Checkered Red and White Shirt" and "The Light in Our Bodies" appeared in *Georgia Review;* "Madre, Guatemala" appeared in *Isthmus;* "39,572" appeared in *Poetry Northwest;* "Photograph" and "Nicaragua, Nicaragua" appeared in *Imagining A Revolution: Poems About Central America;* "Monday Morning" appeared in *Caliope.*

Gerald Weston

"Sweet as Arrowroot" and "Wherever I Looked You Were" appeared in *Windfall*, Winter, 1985; "Out of the Blue" appeared in *Windfall*, Spring, 1986; "Yellow Barn" and "Father William" appeared in *The Muse;* "Cornucopia" and "A Christmas" appeared in *Readings from the Midwest Poetry Festival*, May 8-10, 1986, Vol. 4.

DeWitt
Clinton

I began to take writing seriously, as part of my daily life, while stationed near Chu Lai in South Vietnam, composing a long poem, later published in the first poetry anthology of Vietnam Veterans. Returning to Kansas and graduate study, I concentrated on creative writing between Chaucer and Shakespeare, writing one of the first creative writing master's theses at Wichita State University. After serving as poetry coordinator for the Kansas Arts Commission for a few years, I knew that I wanted to pursue a two year workshop in poetry, so with my wife and young step-daughter, I moved to Bowling Green, Ohio, to pursue an M.F.A. in poetry, and later a Ph.D. in English and Creative Writing.

While at Bowling Green I took an intense interest in the fusion of poetry to history. After reading a number of Central and South American conquistador narratives, I began to write, in 1975, a collection of poetic "improvisations" of history which would later be published as The Conquistador Dog Texts, a multi-volume series of historical improvisations which retold early

1

"Americas" history, culminating, in book length collections, on the Mayan, Aztec and Incan civilizations, the travels of Coronado as well as Mississippi River travellers.

Since living on Milwaukee's East Side, my poetry has taken a much different direction, including a whimsical look at an urban Dracula, poems reflective of conversations, driving and dieting, and exploring what is called "language-oriented" poems, or, for a better "punk" term, new-wave poetry. In addition to these activities, I enjoy editing--so much so that one of my editorial projects is putting this collection of Whitewater poets together. *Salthouse* is a journal I have edited (with a focus on history and poetry) since 1975; and just a few years ago, I co-edited *An Americas Anthology,* a collection of geo-poetic and historical poetry. Right now I'm working on a critical book length study of the contemporary historical poem. My poetry collections include *The Conquistador Dog Texts,* 1976; *The Coyot. Inca Texts,* 1979; *das Illustrite Mississippithal Revisited,* 1983; *Night Jungle Bird Life,* 1983; and *Active Death: Unholy Rhymes,* 1986.

I take pleasure in writing.

So that I'm Athualpa, last Inca Chieftan before Pizzaro and Spanish domination.

So that I can dive, wrapped in golden necklaces, into bottomless Mayan lakes--and experience whatever is down there.

So that I can live as Alvar Nuñez Cabeza de Vaca, lost conquistador, a slave to Indians, in Florida, Mississippi and Texas, sometimes around 1555.

So that I might write as "El Inca," or Garcilaso de la Vega, 1539-1616, first Inca historian.

So that I might know the voice, and body, of Doña Marina, or Malinche, female translator to Hernan Cortez and the Aztecs.

So that I can drift down the Mississippi with Marquette and Joliet.

So that I, too, can walk, delirious, in the Sun, in search for gold, with Coronado.

So that I can feel, in part, the death of Ché Guevara, in Bolivia, in 1967.

2

So that I can come close to my Darkest Powers, as Dracula, on Milwaukee's East Side.

So that I can go back to Vietnam, 16 years later, and recreate a firefight between a North Vietnamese sniper and an American infantry patrol.

So that I can celebrate this leaner body.

So that I can keep my senses by taking pleasure and feeling the absolute delight of poetry.

NIGHT JUNGLE BIRD LIFE

*Ché Guevara's last military
operation in Bolivia,
Oct. 8, 1967*

Night Jungle
Bird Life
Dark Green Trees
A Wet Forest
evening music
A field radio
A small portable fire
The air clearing at night, sleeping
in comfortable caves.
A stringing of flare lines,
The Border Infra-red
Murderous, Beans & Medicine.
Smacking the radio
Night birds
shooing
out.
A flare,
The Whole Place, Lighted
A Sunny Place, an Eclipse
Out of Place,
a penlight, sporadic at night.
The wiping of a Body
as in Good Sex
as in Death
as Now, a radio
Speaking a Horrific
Moment, a defoliation,
Mountainous ravines.
A jaguar crying to sleep.
Coughing an anxiety
a blending with forest birds
so perfect, not to know
who's who, a twilighting,
a gulping drink, a
Coca-Cola
coating the Body.
This is history, historic.
Retrieving land like this

4

is a tactical error
The Whole Continent Knowing
It is not the right Spot
Not pointing the map right
Dancing a way out, a trombone
A saxophone
a flute
A ballet
an orchestral mode
A duet collapsing
Entwined. A jaguar
Mute, long in duration.
A tree fondled.
Subdued lights, shinnying
up a smooth
Coconut.
A Body All Full of Holes
A General Flying A
Helicopter seeing this
Historic body/coupling
Stretched Historic Bodies
The Government
Tracking with
Telescopes.
The couple, in Water
Floating, like Air
Turning, like Meat
A Photograph
A World
Hysteria.

BULLET

Things
are winding
down
& it's
best
to be
thin
now
invisible
space

5

these
bullets
coming in
slow motion
a body's
last orbit
& the
impact
slowly
opening
inwardly
into the body
as if all bullets
have nests
in lovely wet
systems
of body
parts
& the way in
is ecstasy
the bullet
caving
through bone
looking for a
tiny
geography
making fever
spider dances
visions
& then
the nuclear
breaking up
losing all
sense
this
being
a bullet's
ethereal
home.

FEELING ODDLY COLD THEN WINGÉD AS A BAT

But I've no History, say
of Wanting Blood--
nor do I subscribe
to pulpy things--
I'm quite clean,
my brain still
scanning normally--
then Why the Bloody Blokes
do I want to Go Out
& try to Force
the Cursed Thing
once out?

As I said
I'm a Cheerful
lad--mostly smiling,
good at script--
Why such Outlandish
Odd blue things
making me
such a
Wanton
Thing?

I could dine
on a Morgue tonight--
fall drinking down
with Red Cross types--
I've got no class
when the Sun goes down
& yet as I scribble
these meekly thoughts
my mouth does Yawn, nay
not Yawn--
doth Stretch
& Salivate
for some good Body part--
though I'd feel safer
chomping on tin cans--
I don't want to Fly
into some sweet Lady's
Things--I just know
there's more to Life

than acting as a
Wolf, a Bat, a long
Dead Thing--some friend
of Tutankhamen
or Cro-Magnon.

I feel so out of it
So long & Timeless
Nothing New
I read Blake, Dickinson, Hughes
But they only set me Afire
flying like poor Emily,
Hosting the Prophets
or conning God with Crow.

I'm gone--I know it.
Please know I'm quite
delighted--rude--
a kind of punk Stage Presence.

Sometimes my head Lifts
off and Spins Around
in such a Merry
Orbit I am sick
sticking fingers
down those arteries
& Veins--my hand
Extends down in
& I grasp

my Heart, palpitating
it much Faster--Believing
Some Fine Mystery.

O Jeeze--the Floor is
Spinning--my Hands
now do doth Stretch
O Friend
I am a Luminous Being
I Glow like some Strange Thing.

Perchance I'm Something
Delirious--you should
see the Velvety dear Wings--
Curved Blue Teeth,
Nice Soft Cape--
I know it's Odd

but Hell
I'm going through some Phase
I know it's just
some Passing
Thing.

THE BIRDS DO CHIRP THY STILL AND VERY HEART

So near this morning's chirp
blue wingéd, cheery beaks
singing light & springy tunes--
I am adrift--here--in this
black space--nothing to do
but Calm thyself from Night's
run--reminiscing pearly flesh
around thy sharpened teeth--
new mates for life yet separated
until death. I bite
my fingernails, twiddle
my thumbs, listen to bones
crackle as I move my toes
this way, then that way.
O Ennui! 'Tis hard to sleep.
By Nature I'm an insomniac--
a silly phase before my lids
do droop away--what is one
to do all day in black &
sound proofed space, silk pillows at head's rest?
I surely am constrained
from leaping out of here--
I'd vanish--poof!--beGone.
So every saddened Morn I must
Fly back to my blue Grave--be
thankful for night's gifts
& please not brood so deeply
so in dark with light
all radiant about me.

TRAVELLING TO WORK

The two of us count night's slaughter
on the way to work. Each morning
it's darker and darker. I'm afraid

our count isn't always accurate.
Usually the first one has crawled
to the shoulder, so in this morning's

light, I'm the one who usually breaks
the news, in between glances of landscape
and strategies for work. The first one,

often, isn't counted until a second
one is spotted, at the very edge
of our beam--then a second to swerve--

or center our wheels so we don't split
it open anymore. By the time we're both
counting, we can't remember the first.

The third, and nearly always we count
three, is the freshest kill: blood
from skull, mouth, ears, spine, anus.
By then, we know we're almost there.

SNIPER TO POINT
for Dale Ritterbusch

A rifle patrol an oiled barrel
woods green with dangling things
breathing so slight like swimming
through kelp the point walking

backward already sighting a bullet
travelling in such tiny space
followed by two or three more a
free-for-all on the point's chest,

neck opened, an eye sunk, stinging
quite true and deep, now mixed
with electrolytes, platelets,
a busy electrocution

knees falling to earth, a patrol
poised at a tall green tree
a barrage of fire pruning
limb, snake, monkey tail

a thousand rounds in memory
for two who did not quite agree.

THE WAITING ROOM

I have no snakes,
no anacondas, no
mambas to actually
speak of, no Brazilian
leopard's mouth tearing
limb or chest, no Jamaican
sky where banana trees
wait patiently on sun,
on rain, no dead revolutionaries
to mourn, no mountain top
to ascend, no boat or ship
or sea, no landing pad
from orbital flight.
Nothing, you see, of any
consequence. Here I am:
43.05 N. Lat., 87.52 W. Long.
I'm positioned in a one
story brick house, 14 houses
on this side of the block.
I'm in the middle bedroom,
converted to a study, no rug,
though my wife wants one
in here, yet I like the feel
of wood on feet, especially
in the summer, like now.
For better light I've moved
my desk to face two side-
by-side windows, each four
feet by two and a half feet,
with white lace curtains,
modern Venetian blinds,
open, this morning,
for today's cloudy light.
Here's my view. About

eight feet straight out
is my neighbor's south
wall of Cream City brick.
Slightly to the left
is her bedroom window
and window shade,
and no matter what hour,
or season, it's always
drawn down. So I have
no pandas, you see,
nothing Ethopian,
no burst of tears,
no ecstasy, no Jamaican
sky, no funerals today,
no immigrant grandparents
with babuskas, pipe or song.
No faith, no magic, no spells
or superstition--no affairs.
Here's what I've got:
beads of rain collapsing
on two window sills,
the Thursday trash collector,
a few commuters pulling
out from the stop sign.
I predict nothing, absolutely
nothing, will move into the
space between these walls.
Right now all I feel
is the thin slow push
of peristalsis. Outside
I hear a siren, police,
I think. I put my left
hand to my face, like
I'm thinking or something.
Only I'm not. If I stay
here, I'll soon be gazing
down this leopard's mouth,
no strength to pull the jaws
apart, dull the claws or
gouge a hole with blade.
Right now I've planned
no Painted Desert, no
Smokies, no Marianas Trench,

no memories, right now,
of any past, my own, or
yours, no idea at all of what might happen next.
Yet I'll wait, with hunter's
patience, in this small room.

COMING HOME

Outside Chicago we stop by for some Sanka.
It's past mid-afternoon, lunch is digesting
quite nicely, but my back needs a stretch,
so does her's, so we eye this sanitary
Burger-King and think that it'll do just
fine, for our purposes, which is to peep
and wet our throats a little. Sunday
afternoon, border town, only a family
feeding on meat and buns, their sounds
quite like happy cows on grass. Anyway,
we're still all dolled up--red tie,
jackets--as it's still part of the
Holidays. We make a bee line for the
toilets and just as we turn MayITake
YourOrderPlease? We point to the bathrooms,
sheepishly, and I raise a left forefinger
for just a minute. Then we're both
in the bathrooms, so relieved to have
found this off the road place. It doesn't
take either of us long, we're not in there
to do bigger business, so we both look
at each other in the lobby, smiling, and
quite a bit relieved. I ask what'll you
have, dear, and she says--I should have
known--coffee. So it's two Sankas,
creamers and sweet n' lo please. It's
such a small order he doesn't even announce
it on his little mike. I carry the tray
of Sankas to a little white table, there
we both take off our overcoats, as it's
too warm in the car, and warm here, too.
She gets out her Kents. And I swizzle
cream into the steaming paper cup.
We say nice things about the weekend.
The Friday lunch. The Field Museum.

The Chicago Health Club. That night great
veal and egg rolls. The curtain open,
the yellow moon rising above the Lake,
the sky line, the frozen Chicago River.
Then Sunday we check out, and take
Sheridan Drive all the way home.
We see an open carwash and get the car
washed, and then this pleasant drive
home. And as the coffee cools a bit,
you say the weekend isn't quite over,
and smile, and then we leave. A funny
thing happens the next morning--it's
quite early, 4:30 or so, the heater's
on, the radio's on, I've made coffee--then
you know what? All the power goes off in the
house, for about 30, 40 seconds. In the dark,
I think we're going to be murdered, hacked up
bad, a message in blood on our bedroom walls.
And then the lights come back on--and that's
never happened before like that. Then the radio
announcer comes back on, and in a few seconds,
the click of the heater. It feels so good not
to be dead just now.

LONG TIME NO SEE

Well, thanks for asking, my wife and I
are into dieting now, quite seriously,
since we came back from Jamaica. About
50 pounds for me. Over 100 pounds for
her. And we've put over 600 miles on
our indoor bike. Four maybe five times
a week we're either lifting ourselves
up, or pushing something up, or pedaling
to Stevie Wonder's Musiquarium. Friends
have stopped to ask her about when she's
going to stop, and why so much. Some
don't even recognize her. One woman,
suddenly, added up all my lost pounds
at once, and couldn't stop saying how
wonderful it was. You see, last year
we were both into gourmet cooking school
and eating class results every Tuesday

night. In fact, one couple would always
stop by late Tuesdays just to see how
we were, and if we brought home any
extras. We planned, quite seriously,
a gourmet catering service; she in black
skirt, apron; me in a butler's tux. Now?
Well, now we're more impressed with the
odometer on our bike. Food is different,
too. More fish that I've ever imagined.
Chicken with garlic, paprika and lime.
Lots of vegetables, steamed, no butter.
Every kind you can think of. Yogurt
and fruit--none of my fruited trifles
or pecan tortes. All in all, we feel
pretty good. We're both trying on new
sizes. I have to admit it's even fun
to go out shopping. And it's very
interesting to watch other people eat,
especially those who sit close to their
plates. Forks usually always stay in
motion. Whenever I do that now, and sure,
that happens when I've not eaten much,
I nearly always feel hungry right after--
like, let's eat again or something.
The trick is to use an appetizer fork,
put the fork down after about four bites,
sit back, look around and visit some.
Let the old stomach know it's being fed.
Anyway, it's kind of neat. And thanks
for asking. Hey, there's the bus.
You look good too.

THE ANOREXIC MAN
   for Gerry Weston

My own heart beats,
I can see it, there,
right now, standing
wet, cooling off
from the steam,
all this weight
lost, looking in
a new body, in me,

who's there, looking
out, some sixty pounds
thinned, vanished,
a slim, svelte torso
some say gone too
far, toweling off,
drying the mirror,
looking over this
new found body,
a tiny moment,
a flutter, a pulse
I had not seen
before, impossible
under those sweet layers
of fatty stuff, and there,
like it had been there
all along, only now
I can start to see
internal organs move,
this pump, so regular
in beat, I lean over
the bathroom sink, lean
closer to see my own
heart beat, scan a
body quite unknown,
a marvel, some say
a corpse, even still,
something new to look at,
keep an eye on, the face,
never imagining the face
would go, tiny little
pockets, sunken, narrow
jaw, the sweet cheeks
gone to bone, the neck,
swiveling to see new
sinews, lines, muscles
coming out and this,
just now, swallowing,
I see my esophagus
contract, and then
these arms, raise
to pull the muscles
up, skinny drumsticks
on this white meat,

an armpit now so deep,
a shadow, a hole two
three inches depending
how I pivot the right
arm ball and socket,
now taking hands, so
many more blue veins
and bone, spread them
out, on my torso,
counting ribs I didn't
know were there, 6, 7,
a hungry lion, swift
and lean, breathing in
deep to see the new
pectorals, good Lord,
I'm a medical textbook,
plastic sheets, in color,
organs, neurological,
bone, muscle, suddenly
I see completely through,
who is this, looking in,
looking out, a body's
parts so clear in view,
heart, rib, sinew,
a slice of orange,
a brussel sprout,
a 4 oz. slab of veal
passing through, feel
pelvic bone, athletic
thigh, penis, scrotum,
about the same, maybe
larger when everything
else has gone so slim,
knee caps re-defined,
calves holding on to
ankle bones, veins
to toes, who's this,
standing here, looking
in, looking out, this
new found quite
new body?

STUDY QUESTIONS

1. Use the Library to research the life and death (1928-1967) of Ché Guevara. Comparing information of his death to the poem, how does "Night Jungle Bird Life" become an *elegy* for the revolutionary's death in Bolivia?

2. Two *persona* poems, "Feeling Oddly Cold Then Winged As A Bat" and "The Birds Do Chirp Thy Still and Very Heart" are spoken in the voice of Dracula. What makes these poems different from your usual impression of Dracula? Try writing a poem in the voice, or *persona,* of someone famous, or infamous.

3. "Sniper to Point" recreates a firefight in the jungles of Vietnam. What do you know about Vietnam? Ask your relatives to tell you about their experiences, particularly if they were stationed in Vietnam, or saw combat. Try writing a short poem about what they experienced.

4. "Coming Home" and "Long Time No See" are *conversational poems*. Who is the *speaker* talking to in each poem? Discuss how something so normal, as an automobile drive, or waiting for a bus, can be poetic material. Try writing a similar *conversational poem.*

5. "The Anorexic Man" is a *mirror-poem*. What are the issues the speaker is trying to confront? What does he mean by "Who's this,/ standing here, looking/ in, looking out, this/ new found quite/ new body?" Explain the long stanza.

Gay Davidson

> ... if you demand on the one hand the raw material of poetry in all its rawness and that which is on the other hand genuine, you are interested in poetry.

Marianne Moore "Poetry"

This statement makes sense to me as a poet. Like many beginning poets, I was convinced that some subjects were inherently poetic (love, the first snowfall, sunsets) while others were unfit for writing about. So my first poems were highly emotional outpourings, filled with abstract philosophy. It is not that they didn't serve a function. My poetry was my private resort, the diary in which I attempted to articulate and explain my feelings and observations. But as I read more poetry and learned to appreciate poets as diverse as Emily Dickinson and Wallace Stevens, I began to see that, in the right hands, any subject could be written about movingly. This revelation was liberating to me.

Poetry, both the writing and the reading of it, is still therapeutic for me. But I hope to have moved outward to the point that my poetry clarifies feelings for others as well as for myself. Pulling off the sleight of hand necessary to re-create in a reader or listener the same kind of emotion I felt in writing is most difficult but most rewarding. As the poems printed here show, my subject matter remains traditional--people and tributes to people, landscape and place--but my hope is that through my poems the reader is awakened to his or her *own* people and places.

Henry James cautioned writers to be those "upon whom nothing is lost." This seems to me good advice.

CROSSING THE NEWVILLE BRIDGE

I like the river in transition,
the way it drowses midsport
between outboard and ice fishing.

What I fear is the way
it pales, asleep, exposed.
The first ice, clasped at piers,
is like my father's hands
when he falls asleep over T.V.

Home hot from a date
I found him this way once
and, giddy, stuck a plastic lily
on his chest.
I wouldn't do that now.

I like the river in transition,
but am anxious too for the snort
of ice reporting breath to bones,
the ellipses of an interrupted snore.

ON THE TENACITY OF WISCONSIN WILDFLOWERS

Deep as they go
these roots insist.
They will be taken
But they will resist.

Chicory at first demurs
Then hurls itself to earth,
muscles stiff, as if threatened
by a ridiculous law.

The import, tiger lily, feral
as the mustang on the plains,
is easy to take. But once inside,
collapses into itself like a girl.

These are the junkfish of flowerdom,
the silly daisy, the plethora of lace,
the candy corn, the swampy milk,
cornflower, bitter mustard.
These will yield before the rake.

No fight, no spunk, they are
Republican flowers who vote straight
tickets and will go along with you
until you take them home.
Then go sullen, wilt, spit pollen.

All are dying to stay alive.
Their faces wizened and set
by morning. Trancebound as monks,
they sour themselves, they gloat.

ELEGY

The sun is finally out today.
At dawn I recall
how you came home, the urban hunter,
brown bags stuffed with
purloined treasure,
fancy teas and crabmeat,
spices I still use today.

Delightedly, you'd pounce,
laughing, your tired, slim
shoulders curving like a
bird's wing around
our illicit spoils.
You'd bring up, laughing,
plastic flowers, and one time, caviar.

Clapping, I'd expect a rabbit
or a string of purple scarves.
Laughing, we'd take our
conspiracy to bed while
the sun broke out in
splinters behind the elm.

DRUMLIN

Over the drumlin
where someone has chosen to live
and I have found the right place to die,
hangs Venus, November's evening star.

In the middle of my town life, I pass
this drumlin twice a day. Heart too big
in love or in rage, worry like paper cuts,
niggling, non-lethal.

Give me no pretty preening pear tree.
I want instead the bitter-fisted country
apple, buckshot tough, the German
names on mailboxes, even, or leaning
like country headstones.

Tonight the seven sisters hang on stems,
ripe, low for plucking, watered by the gourd.
I have driven and driven down the belly of this land,
pulled by the moon which holds an impossible star
like no mother ever held a child.

Now, fullness a lump in my throat,
I want to stop, shag out over this field,
sit silently a spell in this good gathering.

THIRTY

She is counting the rings on her wrist
as in gauging the age of the pine
or in plying the palmist's art--
How many lovers? Children? How many times wived?

Here, geography and destiny are intertwined.
In this hand, barbed wire cut another mouth that shouts
and pains like stigmata when the sun lets down.

She ate dirt twice in the Kansas field.
Once when she had squared the corner,
ridged the oats from west to east,
and when the crop was shaken,
came the ghost of dust unbid.
To close the throat as tight as shocks,
to fill the septum like the tall white bins.

She is paralyzed as by second thoughts of anything--
marriage, childing, a mortgage against Spring,
grounded by hands like lightning rods,
a dowager barn in one last curtsy to the courting prairie wind.

WRITING THE GUTS OUT

These stringy things, poems,
are mostly nestled in deep,
while tougher rind, the zest
of everyday spoilage, waste,
lies nearer, easier to reach.

The knife will sometimes take a plunge
that surprises--a twist, a new mouth
for the flickering candle of inspiration.
You guess that's okay--let 'er slide.
Just as long as you get the guts out.

Never thinking the more you gash,
stand aside, admire with the lights out
that sometimes less is not so much more.
Sometimes less is less in
poems, pumpkins, guts.

HEAD HUNTING

Laying a furrow open with a practiced shoe:
"This time of year the hunting is most urgent.
The smallest shower sends them climbing up like clover.
We've got to be there when they come."

I leaned into March wind like a pack of blooded hounds,
expecting gems to have sprouted where plain dirt once lay.
Bent, he dawdled something on his tongue, mind poised,
looking like a badger or a raccoon fishing
in the moonlight that was noon.

"Don't do this that I'm doing; farmers now plant
poisons in their fields." He showed me where
the head sat thin and pale
as a thumbnail or a shell
against his lower teeth.

"An arrowhead," I murmured.
A limber span of motion and
a deer just free of winter hide
split shadow into sun.

Choked, I blundered into blackest loam,
and sank with every lunge.
"And early as anything," he said,
lifting me to firmer fencerow.

Each time I said, "Look here."
Each time he walked the ridges,
spat, and ran a finger down the stone.
"No," but patiently, and with a tale

That led me on to think of bogs,
acres of ducks, and the river
before it ever dreamed of water.

SETTING OUT

Their names have tangled at the roots.
She wants to rip them clean, set hers apart.

In her dust-deviled wake,
raked through the heart,
I bury a prayer in every mound,
pat down, and follow.

Holding her end of the conversation
taut, she shimmers as in memory,
red face furled; scarf a semaphore
I can't bear to read.

They can't set straight the row it seems.
Dug up at last, words break hard as clods.
She talks of bread resented, a bed unshared,
life of her own after forty years.

She holds that she will leave him
Before the corn comes in.
My blood rushes toward her,
and toward him, my father,
her husband, and, at last, a man.

25

RECONNAISSANCE
To Mother

From the depth of my blue studies
I am raised by the heat of your gaze.
Yours is a familiar trance.
You are performing reconnaissance.

For this moment, my peach-fuzzed lip,
the ellipse of my jaw--are not my own.
Perhaps Aunt Elsie, your sister,
peers through my borrowed hazel eyes.

I have seen you, like Solomon, hold a newborn,
naming part by part his debt to kin.
As a child myself, I did not understand
the mystery of your trance, asking "What did I get?"

I thought of slate-like Indian hair that fell,
a creek at floodtime over logjams.
I hoped for at least the Irish skin,
the laughter like a flight of birds.

Surfacing as if from a daze,
You nodded, spoke in measured pace,
As if you were suddenly brought to light:
"Yes. Yes. From the Smith side, the overbite."

SWIMMING WITH MY MOUTH

The baleen whale scours
the ocean with its mouth
wide open until it finds
the food it needs.

I, too, must swim
with my mouth wide
open. There is no snail
or krill or weed I cannot use.

I must engulf the trivial,
the flotsam and jetsam of the
wrecks, the grief, the days
when I feel beached, the
storms and seines and seiche.

To feed that voracious appetite
I must sift and glean,
must patrol ceaselessly,
grazing these waters.

SLOWPITCH: RUNNING MANTRA #1

I am running you out of my life.
Like a dirty joke my knees were drawn.
Now as strong as outfielder's arm.
With town riff-raff whose literary quip is,
"As Shakespeare says, 'That sucker's out.'"
But who know as much of love
as either he or we did.

They wonder at the way I play
Who never knows the score, the inning,
the call on that last pitch.
And I'm awash in the purpling trees,
the bordering woods, the swallows'
wings as they and the sun salute
a brilliant catch. I heed the
voice of big rocks bumping brown
water that chooses to meander
despite town engineers.

We cheer the illiterate wisdom
when the diabetic brittle as kindling
is taken out at first, and
the game goes on in grace.
The fat girl who can't run
is face on a bobble that looks so real
only she and God know the difference.

Jailbirds and jailbait, drunks and cons,
bullies, bigmouths, boys whose voices
tell their bodies who they are.
Our cleats bare feet encrusted with mud.
Uniforms are skins and shirts.
Children whose pop-bottle arms
and coltish legs cause them to
tumble at the lightest tag.

A bristling, tattooed United Nations
drinking democratic Bud as Sunday
goes spinning toward Monday.
The only rules: no politics
                      no race
                      no romance
And nothing that passes for lingua franca
In a well-dressed place.

Above all, no philosophy:
You run your reasons and I mine: we keep the code.
The eye is on lopsided ball; the ear whatever music
made by whack of cloth on wood, the slap of the catch.
These solid things that no one yet misunderstood.

STUDY QUESTIONS

1. How do the specific *details* in "On the Tenacity of Wisconsin Wildflowers" help you to see these flowers? Find several examples of *personification* and explain how Davidson has brought animation to these flowers. Explain the lines "they are / Republican flowers who vote straight / tickets and will go along with you / until you take them home."

2. The title of one poem is "Drumlin." Look up this term and explore how Davidson has created *images* of landscape. Make a list of details she uses to describe this drumlin.

3. "Head Hunting" uses *dialogue* which is more often found in fiction. How does dialogue help you to more easily experience this poem? Try replacing the dialogue with *exposition*. How is the poem different?

4. What is "Swimming with My Mouth" about? The poem is an *analogy*, but what is the comparison? The poem is also a *metaphor* for direction in life. Can you explain the metaphor? What is it that the speaker must "patrol ceaselessly"?

5. Compare "SlowPitch: Running Mantra #1" to Dale Ritterbusch's "44." Both are examples of *sports poetry*, yet how are the two baseball poems completely different in *forms* as well as in *theme*?

Ron Ellis

My interests as a poet extend from the printed poem through performance poetry to the fusion of poetry with other arts: music, cinema, video. Although in my origins and emphasis the written poem takes precedence, I love to experiment. A few years after I published my first poem in Commonweal (1965), musician Stefan Sylvander and I composed an intermedia piece called "Psychles" which fused poetry, film, slides, concrete sound, and electronic music. Involvement in teaching full time at the University of Wisconsin-Whitewater, the voter registration movement, the anti-war movement, working in absentia on a Ph.D. at Cornell, and raising four children put severe constraints on my creative life in those years; very few poems got written and even fewer got published. Yet Stefan and I created the "Kids Suite" (1970), with live sounds of our kids, synthesizer, clips from home movies, and slides. In the seventies I was experimenting with the use of media in the college classroom, getting grants and equipment, working out an alternative terminal degree with the Union Graduate School, and writing very little--all these things seemed to be leading somewhere, however.

By 1977 I was peaking with media: in January I presented "Space Suite" (16mm film, 35mm slides, electronic synthesizer, live dancers) in collaboration with Marion Garber at Virginia Commonwealth University. In July I presented in the Fiske Planetarium in Boulder, Colorado, an extravaganza titled "The Energy Called Female" (dancers, jazz ensemble, tape, 16mm film, 35 mm slides), a distillation of the life of Brandy Wood. Allen Ginsburg attended, enjoyed the piece, but said that Brandy hadn't "spent enough time in the void."

Back in Wisconsin I continued to write poetry, and became deeply involved for a few years with a "commune" called Rock Ridge. It was OK insofar as it led to some good poems, particularly "The Power of the Doe". The media roll continued: from 1978-80 I produced "Hiroshima Ma Honte" (double 16mm projection, tape collage), "Stretching" (double 16mm projection, tape collage), and "The Whaling Witch" (16mm film, synthesizer). In 1980 "Dead Air" was printed in *Poetry Northwest,* an event which reaffirmed the central role of written poetry in my life.

But I remained fascinated with intermedia. In the same year I produced at UW-Whitewater a sestina I had written, "Venus Sings to Pioneer" (poem, synthesizer, flute), in cooperation with the Astronomy Open House sponsored by the Physics Department. At this time I was working with Al Jewer, a flutist, computer programmer/technician, and sound engineer; the collaboration continues. In 1981 we produced "Song to Sophia" (poem, synthesizer, natural sounds, flute) and, in 1983, "White Shadow Quartet," (choral reading, percussion, flute, multiple 16mm projection), performed in "How the Poet Imagines Nuclear War," an evening in the series, "Perspectives on Nuclear War," sponsored by the UW-Whitewater Physics Department.

The quartet employed four live voices alternately reading phrases I had culled from lectures on the physical, psychological, technological, and military aspects of nuclear war. The voices were matched by four projectors without sound throwing 50's images of cultural stereotypes. That evening marked the first performance of my poetry by "Random Sample," a rock band Al and I had been practicing with in his basement sound studio. By April of '84 we had worked together well enough to perform, as part of the Sixth Annual Poetry Festival at UW-Whitewater, several of the *Pratyeka Cantos,* a major work-in-progress. The impetus for the cantos came from my experience at the Naropa Institute's *Jack Keruoac School of Disembodied Poetics,* which put

30

on a mammoth Kerouac conference in the summer of '82. I workshopped with Ginsberg, Ted Berrigan, Michael McClure, and Herbert Huncke, and listened to Ferlinghetti, Kesey, Corso, Holmes, Waldman, Di Prima.

To date eight of the cantos are published or forthcoming. In Spring '85 we formed the *Chamber Rock Ensemble*, and there is a cassette album out now, of poem-experiments involving computer, synthesizer, and rock band formats, called *Open My Eyes*, which includes a few of the cantos.

In November 1985 I studied for three weeks with William Stafford and Alvin Lucier at the Atlantic Center for the Arts in Florida. The workshop with Stafford reaffirmed the unique primacy of the written word in my work; the sessions with Alvin took me way out there to places you can find by listening to the album, particularly to "Macadamia Nut," inspired by the Lucier album, *I Am Sitting in a Room*.

What else? My poems appear in NRG, BORDER CROSSINGS, QUIXOTE, CREAM CITY REVIEW, VELOCITIES, THE WISCONSIN ACADEMY REVIEW, STAR LINE, INDRA'S NET, THE NEW JERSEY POETRY JOURNAL, TAURUS, THE SUCARNOCHEE REVIEW, SOW'S EAR, among many others. Although I've gotten away from the visual media in the last several years, the drive toward synthesis is still there.

SCENES OF GREEN LIGHT

i

My brother stared through the tractor exhaust
at the rippling land and the trembling clouds
as he drove us out to the field. My father
stood on the drawbar, narrowing his eyes against
the cigarette that seemed to cut furrows in his face
as he looked to where the windrows were strung
like fat cables on the east slope. I stood
in the wagon, my knees bent to take its lurching,
my hands firm on the creaking endgate.
The hay-sling rope felt hard as a bead of weld
under my ankle-high workshoes. In the fence-row
tangled with brush and barbed-wire, bleached posts
slanted where they rotted, jutting out of fieldstone
once hauled by horses with the stoneboat made of
rough planks and strap iron we scrapped that year.

ii

We were the burning end of the slow fuse, the windrow.
The steady pulling haunted my brother's daydream.
The stubble popped against the tires and the smell
of cured hay was dense as smoke. Brittle leaves
flaked like ashes and fell in our collars as the hayloader's
tine-studded hardwood arms pushed up the alfalfa
ribbon my father caught and pitched to where
I clambered as the wagon slanted and shifted.
He called for help, it was so thick on the low side
of the hill; together we sank our forks and pulled.
He gasped as the clot gave way; I flushed
with a new heat as he called me strong.

iii

The sling-load of hay, long stems streaming back,
soared to the half-full mow, the carrier clicking
on the hangars my father nailed to the peak of the roof.
I pulled the trip-rope; the sling burst open,
the load fell with a dry, rushing sound,
puffing leaves that drifted down as we climbed
the ladder. The hard, worn ridges of the axe-trimmed rungs
stung my yellowed callouses. I stalled on the oak
cross-beam, crouching in the hot, still air,

32

and then jumped into the mow so the dust churned and glowed
in slits of light. I tugged against a knot of hay;
my father showed me how to pull apart the layers
which caught the light in green flashes
as he pitched them against the wall. I saw
the yellow spiders retreat in quivering webs
and the green light darken in mazes of stems and leaves.

WAVE FORMS

Hickory nuts lie like seashells
whose oxygen molecules reveal
a half-million year cycle
of the earth's magnetic field.
Putting down the magazine, looking up

at what must be the magnetosphere,
I imagine charged particles
spinning like shattering hickory husks,
"mischief that can make cab-drivers in Alaska
obey dispatchers in New Jersey."

Here a chipmunk totes a nut. Up there
solar flares generate waves called ELF
that circle the earth continually.
We generate them, too,
send them to subs hemispheres apart.

I can hear tides of wind. It is said
when the length of those waves
equals the circumference of the earth,
they are the same as alpha waves
that lap the shore of mind.

Around me leaves tumble curled and dried.
I close my eyes to the sun rippled
by lattices of hickory, imagine
solar wind colliding with earth,
shock waves piercing the boundary layer

so the magnetotail weaves curtains
on the night side, sheets of red
or yellow-green that curl and fold.
From space they appear as ovals of auroral light.
Time to stroll home in the oncoming dark.

WIND GAUGE

"calm: smoke rises vertically"

and curls, floating folds that stretch
like the long afternoon,
variations of light playing out,
thoughts like steeping tea.

"1-12 mph: you can just feel wind on face"

just in time to bring me back,
imagine erotic breath.
Leaves rock on a branch
leisurely as yachts.

"13-24: raises dust or loose paper"

Mice skitter above the ceiling.
Must get my house in order.
Might answer that long letter.
Snow-devils swirl across the road.

"25-30: gusty: wires whistle"

Hang on to the door.
Let me get that TV.
Hard luck for the poor.
Good of you to stop by.

"30-40: heavy wind: whole trees in motion"

but they can't walk away.
Hard to walk against.
Long-stemmed cosmos bend, go flat.
No, your cigar isn't much of a threat.

"40-72: tornado watch: loose objects dangerous"

So you say it's a matter of will.
This jasmine is especially good.
I say without form there is no desire.
My, there goes a week's worth of trash.

"73-120: hurricane: aircraft grounded, take immediate shelter"

Listen to the knick-knacks knock.
Goodness, here comes your ash-tray.
Shall we ponder in the cellar?
Or stay here till the roof lifts off?

"120-200: major tornado: all structures endangered"

We forgot to open all the windows!
Here, let me get those bricks.
You've got a point about emptying the mind.
Let's just stare where the wall was.

"200-800: cataclysm: shelter in tunnels if available"

There's just a little tea left.
All that sonic booming.
Are you sure you need a light?
You've passed me just the handle of your cup.

"800-11,160,000: earth out of orbit, be alert for further bulletins"

The air is thick with bric-a-brac.
Beats staying at home.
Can I get you something
for those hemhorraging eyes?

"11,160,000-669,600,000: solar wind--you can just feel void on face"

Puts one in an expansive mood.
Arthur? haven't seen him in eons.
Care for a spoonful of Jupiter?
You look distinctive in ions.

"calm: smoke rises vertically--"

So glad you came--then we agree
the greatest form has no shape.
We must get together again,
weather permitting.

THE POWER OF THE DOE

i

Think of it as a film run backwards:
condensing clouds of dust, the game warden's car
moves in reverse on our valley road,
guided by the doe's glazed eyes.

ii

The warden's hands seem to follow the rope
that unties her from the trunk.
She pulls him by the hand with her hind leg,
slithers across the grass,
feeling the way with her tongue.

iii

We who were already forgetting
step back as in a hesitant dance,
in light no longer failing,
to the place where blood gathers.

iv

You and I in hunted love
see the deer begin to twitch.
Our daughter of seventeen, never so far,
has come so close to watch.

v

Blood flows up the tawn coat
into the waiting skull.
Doe hairs cling to my damp clothes.
You and I exchange a look,
finality draining into shock.

vi

Laura backs to where the others stare.
The silence fades into crescendoes of echo
as the reflexes sharpen to total spasm,
gunshot birth.

36

vii

The warden aiming received the bullet.
He holsters his gun
and with his palm face out
warns the children to come.

viii

They come snowballing hope.
He strokes the paralyzed flank,
touches the scab that creases the spine,
explains like a shaman in his reversed tongue.

ix

The doe slides up to my sagging embrace.
It's a long climb to the high field.
We're chilled and wet; you prop my arm.
We'll stop at the stream.

x

Her black hooves, layered with white,
are couched on watercress.
She won't drink.
You raise her white-whiskered mouth.

xi

The water erupts, sprays us
on its way to her. She's getting strength in those
two good legs
that churn against my grasp--
we can even laugh.

xii

Our grotesque baby. I'm holding her
belly up, her long legs sticking out all over.
She's wide-eyed, the lashes long and curved,
the ears laid low. There's rough footing
on these ridges. A stray dog circles and snaps.

xiii

The house, the yard, the children there
getting just a little younger, grow small.
My arms strain to keep her, but she's
getting lighter, the curve of her spine
rising in the hoop of my arms.

xiv

We rest among rock and sod,
oak and birch.
The doe is calm, certain, intent.
She turns to watch the dog.
We could be content.
In the last ravine she squirms, writhes,
wrenches out of my grip, down to flat rock.
I hear the hooves of a great avenging buck--
it's her heart--beating primal terror!

xvi

I seize her, clamp the oval of her chest.
Her front legs flail, spittle froths her mouth--
she bellows, arching her neck, cries so hoarse,
so deep, greater than my rage to possess--
she drags me, staggering, clinging, into the brush.

xvii

She releases me.
I step back to where
decision softens, the letting go,
our voices fingering new words.

xviii

Our hands join.
We move among blueberry, honeysuckle,
under hickory whose leaves shine
the afternoon's climbing light.

xix

The doe waits for days in that quiet
and then lifts, twisting, soaring,
to the high field where she incants
a sliding, leaping dance.

xx

The charmed bullet unearths
and sings to splice the severed nerve,
to mate with its shell of brass--
the hunter recoils amazed.

xxi

Think of it as the last, frozen frame,
or even a picture on an urn:
you and I hiking toward morning,
remembering the blood, the cry, the quiet.

ADDITION

We walked across the lawn that was once
a grain field to the fieldstone house
I used to play in, where box elders grew
among plaster, old canning jars, and crumbling
harness gear--the shell
rebuilt now
as my father's house.

He showed me how he was facing
the added wing with stones he had gathered
from the fence rows: with more care
than the homesteaders once took
in burying granite and limestone whole
in those thick walls, he placed
a black gneiss so the grain was right,
hefted the sledge, and swung, his motion
stiffer, his face more lined than I remembered.
He touched the opened, glittering halves
with his calloused thumb
and told me he liked finding the hidden patterns.

I see him on the fence-rows I used to hike along,
between fields he used to farm:
he pulls stones out of wild raspberry
and flaking barbed wire tangles,
lifts them into the Ford pickup--or
he rests in the shade of scrub trees,
judging how much more weight
the squat tires can bear.

Once we sat on the stones, resting
next to rows of oats we had cut and shocked.
There was the sun and the sweat,
the elm trees were still living, rustling;
we sat, the future working inside me,
my father picking at yellow stubble,
as if by that he could hold off
the auction that was sure to come.

We never talked much. But his placing
of stone to stone, his opening
the seals of the earth,
tells me I must join word to word,
deed to deed,
live worthy of my father's house.

RACCOON

I watch the mechanic pry a dried eye
from the suspension. With the car aloft
I remember how the other night we laughed
sitting so close to the screen
the ghostbusters looked flat.
Then drinks, the odd choice of a vegetarian
restaurant ("doesn't seem to go with special effects"),
the food fresh and carefully washed--driving home
there wasn't time to hit the brakes,

just to glimpse
the raccoon running
amiably as fast as it can--
the skull shatters instantly, the spine twisting
snaps in this mad cavort, bouncing under
the floorboards, how the rear axle thuds
beast we abort--traffic coming
we cry out
carrying the eye now ours.

40

A FORMULA

Touch a milky, fiery opal.
Hold it up to your eye and feel
the pull of the full moon

which in that fire-frosted stone
you turn between
thumb and forefinger

is a snowball the children roll,
their voices like cream
with laughing.

Now step through the glass
and watch them scrape snow
from blackened grass,

handing it up
to make walls crested
with the last flush of sunset.

Go under the arch
they stood on chairs to reach;
speak praise

as their candles, red and green,
inflame the frigid sills
they carved.

Lie down.
The cold bathes you.
As the children speak

you see how the walls lift
to the touch
of the brightest star.

PRESERVES

I liked to malinger in the cellar,
pick at flaking whitewash on the fieldstone walls,
poke under musty gunnysacks, or handle
cast-off tools whose uses I didn't understand.
Sometimes a mouse ran along a beam.
I gazed at rows of pale fruits and dark meats--
later we would fling them all into the dump,

41

the glass spattering and the smells flooding up
from heaps of rusted cans, the wrecked buckboard,
the Model T wheels, and a dead calf--
in one jar I saw the stirring of forbidden life.

"I can't remember now just when
I put up those preserves," Old Lady Dibble said
as she dragged cornflakes into our bowls
with her spotted, faltering hand. She insisted
there were no mice in the house, even after
we sifted droppings out of the flour.
My father made sure he tore out the rusted bin
before mother came from selling the house in town.

I kept the jar as secret as my flesh
that swelled against coveralls; those plump
little beasts cruised along the curving sides
or peeled off into the murky broth. Yet I was busy
learning feeding, milking, field-work
that Old Man Dibble had done alone
(we could hear the leather straps creaking
on his wooden leg); every day we had to scour
barn-gutters brimming with wet manure.

When the old man's Hupmobile threw a rod
he fitted a piece of box elder into the cylinder;
it ran fine on five. Once he told us,
"Now that dog, when he's dead, he's dead,
but me, I gotta go to hell yet."
They finally moved out, but the hay-wagon
they borrowed overturned at the end of our road.
As we helped I hummed, "Hallelujah I'm a bum."
The polished Victrola was wrecked. Old Lady Dibble
cried as she picked steel needles out of the gravel.

The next time I looked the jar had come to a
cold rolling boil of hunching, starving maggots.
I took it under my shirt to the smoke-house
where we dumped coal-stove ashes. Thistles crowded
the doorway. Corroded hooks stuck from cracked beams
bleached where shingles had fallen through.
The smell of old curing hung in the sunlight.
I lifted the jar high and shattered it,
then got out as those multitudes twisted in the grit.

SPIN-OFF

Firing dead chickens at airplanes
is part of a test program to ensure structural quality
and thus make air travel safer.
The idea of a bird, even a small one,
damaging an airplane is not to be taken lightly.
A specially-trained government team
visits chicken farms to pick up hens
whose egg production has fallen to a critical point.
The birds are easy to handle since they have lived
in wire cages and have never touched the ground.
Their last ride to The Southwest Research Institute
is uneventful and their death is painless.
The poultry are shot from compressed air guns
at windshields and engines fastened to the ground.
"Passenger plane engines must be able to ingest
seventy-five four pound birds without falling,"
says Bill Beckwill, senior engineer at the institute.
"But the technicians don't like the chickens," he says.
"They have a bad odor and are messy as well.
On a more technical level, it's hard getting
repeatable results, since chickens vary so
in size and weight." A solution Beckwill
and his colleagues have come up with
is bird substitutes--cylindrically shaped jelly-like
forms that mimic the balance of water and air
in a real bird. They are awaiting FAA approval
for use of the substitute birds on a nationwide basis.

STUDY QUESTIONS

1. "Scenes of Green Light" is a *reminiscence* of a hay harvest. How has the *speaker* helped you to see this experience? List the specific *details* which make this poem visual. Is there a *message* in this reminiscence?

2. "Wing Gauge" creates a progression of different winds, from "calm" to "solar wind." Yet each category offers unexpected insights. How does this technique of surprise hold your interest in the poem? What would you have written for "40-72: tornado watch: loose objects dangerous"?

3. Read "Power of the Doe" several times. What makes this a *lyric?* What makes it also *dramatic* and *narrative?* Discuss the *emotions* explored in this poem.

4. "Preserves," "Addition" and "Scenes of Green Light" all celebrate childhood experiences. Recall an experience from your past (a simple experience, nothing too dramatic) and try to design a poem with either a *narrative* or *lyrical* form.

5. Try to identify *sarcasm* and *humor* in "Spin-Off." Define sarcasm and discuss how it applies, and where, in this poem.

Ray
Griffith

I enjoy living and working in other countries and feel lucky I
have been able to teach at schools in four extremely diverse
regions of the world: India, Korea, England, and Australia.

Some of these poems are from the days I lived in India and
taught at Punjab Agricultural University in Ludhiana. Punjab is
the homeland of the Sikh religion, and all male Sikhs are named
Singh, like Hazara Singh and Amrjit Singh, and sometimes with a
clan name added, like Satjit Singh Grewal.

Narangwal was one of the Sikh villages in which I lived; I
was always fascinated with the wild peacocks that foraged in the
field during the day and returned each night to roost in the
trees in the village. In April and May, the hottest season of the
year, Punjab Agricultural University began classes two hours
earlier to avoid the heat of the middle of the day; as I walked
through town at dawn on my way to work, I used to see the
balloon-sellers leaving their homes.

Khajuraho, far south of Punjab, is the site of over thirty sandstone temples decorated with elaborate carved reliefs that are famous for their beauty and depiction of sensuality. These Khajuraho temples are considered the finest examples of medieval Hindu sculpture.

The feature of poetry that attracted me to it most originally was no doubt melody--all the various types of sound repetition that make poetry musical--meter and rhyme and alliteration and assonance and consonance and refrains. I was a great admirer of Edgar Allen Poe at a very young age, and I still am. His poems are incantations--almost hypnotic in their use of repetition. I suppose melody stuck in my mind when I was very young as what differentiated prose and poetry.

But in the twentieth century that melodic tinkle has been found most commonly in the works of lyricists--Noel Coward, Cole Porter, Lorenz Hart, Alan Jay Lerner--and in humorous verse--Ogden Nash, Phyllis McGinley, Dorothy Parker. Some of their subjects can be bitter but they all labor heavily to make the effect light. They want their poetry to cut all ties with the ponderous and the pompous, with super-self-seriousness, and to float free. They want to blow up balloons of words and let them fly away. That's what I'd like to do if I could.

ROSES

The world's favorite blossom as everybody knows
Is that prickly-stemmed, showy flowered shrub called the rose.
But more common than in gardens, the rose also grows
In literary works, in rose poems and rose prose--
Roses that are worldly, roses epistolic.
All the many roses with meanings symbolic:
The rose as beauty, as elegance, as bliss,
The rose as mortality and death's final kiss,
The rose of Cupid and of lacy Valentine love,
The rose of martyrdom and of divine love.
The fertile rose in the verse from Isaiah that goes,
"The desert shall rejoice and blossom like the rose."
And there's Greek poet Sappho, who with no furbelows,
Said the queen of all flowers must be the rose.

The Arabs thought the rose fit a masculine pose,
As did Shakespeare himself in those huge folios
Where Antony wears "the rose of youth" that glows
And Richard the Second is "this sweet lovely rose."
Poor Hamlet before he began to disintegrate
Was "the expectancy and the rose of the fair state."
Juliet compares Romeo, not long after they meet,
To a rose that by any name would still smell sweet.
But sweet rose men can also meet defeat
Like in "La Belle Dame Sans Merci" of John Keats;
The knight at arms there, confused and dithering,
Has a rose on his cheek that is fast withering.

Women, too, are roses, at least to their beaux,
As in Robert Burns' "My Luve Is Like a Red Red Rose."
Tennyson's young hero is completely overawed
By the rose cheeks and rose mouth of his lovely Maud.
Then there's little buds still in their swaddling clothes
Like that "li'l feller" who's "mighty lak' a rose."

Poets like Herrick who believe we decompose
For a lifetime before those final death throes
Advised us to live the seize-the-day-way
And always "Gather ye rosebuds while ye may."
Herbert looked at the rose with a mournful sigh
And warned the mortal flower, "Thou must die."
Omar Khayyam, too, stressed death and decay
When he asked the whereabouts of "the Rose of Yesterday."

But poets like Vaughan thought that Heaven bestows
On the rose a sure sign of the spirit's repose;
It has within its petals the power to bring release,
For "the Rose that cannot wither" is "the flower of Peace."
Algernon Charles Swinburne, however, discloses
That really "no thorns go as deep as the rose's,"
Which means be very wary whom you trust
For love can be even "more cruel than lust."
The rose had many meanings for William Butler Yeats,
And in one poem it signifies the Irish Free State;
He tells the Irish people if they want to be free
Only their own blood "can make a right Rose Tree."

Objecting to such symbols was the late Gertrude Stein,
Who tried to freshen up the rose in her most famous line.
With her syntax bizarre so the reader doesn't doze,
She insisted that "A rose is a rose is a rose."

But the literature of roses still grows and grows;
We think the rose is a poem and a poem is a rose,
Like this ancient verse in its latest version yet
From the 1986 elementary school set:
"Roses are red, clover is green,
You have the shape of a washing machine."
I guess as long as any poet anywhere composes,
Everything's coming up roses . . . and roses . . . and roses. . . .

ROOMS

There are rooms to start up in
Rooms to start out in
Rooms to start over in
Rooms to lie in
Rooms to lie about in
Rooms to be lied to about being lied about in
Rooms to lay away in
Rooms to lay up in
Rooms to lay over in
Rooms to lie low in
Rooms to lie about being laid up in
Rooms to be put in
Rooms to be put up in
Rooms to be put up to in

Rooms to be put up with in
Rooms to be put up with for putting on in
Rooms to put down in for putting up with being put off
     in putting forth in
Rooms to turn in in
Rooms to be turned in in
Rooms to be turned on in
Rooms to be turned down in
Rooms to be turned around in
Rooms to be turned over in
Rooms to be overturned in
Rooms to turn away in when being held off in
Rooms to be turned upon in for turning up turned out in
Rooms to hold back in
Rooms to hold in in
Rooms to hold out in
Rooms to hold on in
Rooms to hold forth on in about being held off in
Rooms to be held down in
Rooms to be upheld in
Rooms to withhold in when being held up in
Rooms to sit up in
Rooms to sit down in
Rooms to be set down in
Rooms to sit about in
Rooms to set about in
Rooms to set out in
Rooms to sit in on in
Rooms to be set aside in
Rooms to be set upon in
Rooms to sit up in to be set off in
Rooms to be set back in for sitting out in
Rooms to be set up in for being sat on in for sitting back in
Rooms to be upset in
Rooms to give in
Rooms to give in in
Rooms to take in in
Rooms to be taken in in
Rooms to be mistaken in
Rooms to be mistaken about in
Rooms to take over in
Rooms to be overtaken in
Rooms to take up with in
Rooms to be taken up on in

Rooms to give in in about being taken up in
Rooms to give over to being taken on in
Rooms to be taken off on in for being taken aback in
    about being given away in
Rooms to give up in

DEWEY DECIMAL

Thomas Dewey had great political acumen
And ran for president against Harry S Truman.
George Dewey sank a whole Spanish flotilla,
Became admiral and was the hero of Manilla.
John Dewey's pragmatism was most impressive
And he made our public schools progressive.
But all these feats are really infinitesimal
Compared to Melvil Dewey and his famous
    Dewey Decimal.

Library of Congress call numbers phooey,
Give me the decimals of Melvil Dewey.

FERNS

The Marsh Fern, the Wood Fern, the Pond Fern,
The Japanese Painted Fern, a multicolored frond fern,
The Interrupted Fern, an easy to discern fern,
The Boston Fern, a pedestal and urn fern.
The Fishtail Fern, the Oriental Brake Fern,
The Massachusetts Fern, or Bog Fern,
The New York Fern, the Silver Leaf Fern,
The Brittle Bladder Fern, the Log Fern.
The Walking Fern, a tip-propagating fern,
The Mother Fern, a self-duplicating fern,
The Climbing Fern, the Beach Fern, the Cliff Fern,
Ebony Spleenwort, which is a very stiff fern,
The Male Fern, a traditional vermifuge fern,
The Mexican Tree Fern, an absolutely huge fern.
The Bird's-Foot Fern, the Bird's-Nest Fern,
The Ostrich Fern, the Feather Fern,
The Hen-and-Chickens Fern, the Hedge Fern,
The Felt Fern, the Leather Fern.
The Christmas Fern, a bright evergreen fern,
The Spinulose Shield Fern, a very seldom seen fern,

50

The Marginal Shield Fern, a spores along the edge fern,
Sierra Cliff Brake, a grows upon a ledge fern.
The Rabbit's-Foot Fern, the Hare's-Foot Fern,
The Squirrel's-Foot Fern, the Claw Fern,
The Elk's-Horn Fern, the Hart's-Tongue Fern,
The Deer Fern, the Bear's-Paw Fern.
The Royal Fern, a likes it moist and shady fern,
Like Goldie's Fern and the Northern Lady Fern,
The Resurrection Fern, a revives in the rain fern,
The Broad Swamp Fern, the Virginia Chain Fern,
Mrs. Cooper's Lip Fern, a grows where it's dry fern,
The Shasta Fern, a likes to live high fern.
The Petticoat Fern, the Verona Lace Fern,
The Button Fern, the Cloak Fern,
The Venus-Hair Fern, the Ribbon Fern,
The Locust Fern, the Oak Fern.
The Staghorn Fern, a tree-dwelling air fern,
The Bristle Fern, the Delta Maidenhair Fern,
The Sensitive Fern, a deeply indented fern,
The Licorice Fern, the Common Hay-Scented Fern.
The Skeleton Fern, the Rib Fern,
The Holly Fern, the Ladder Brake Fern,
The Five-Fingered Fern, the Hand Fern,
The Wart Fern, the Rattlesnake Fern.
Bracken, a knows no enclosures fern,
The Grape Fern, a grows without croziers fern,
The Cinnamon Fern, a florists' give-away fern,
The American Shield Fern, another bouquet fern,
Purple Spleenwort, which is really a blue fern,
And the Asparagus Fern, which is not a true fern.

KHAJURAHO

With the rains the jungle green waves lustrous.
On a clearing of coarse grass
Exposed to a sun half the width of the sky
A buff temple quavers
Amid shimmering waves of monsoon heat.
Musicians carved in sandstone on the walls
Pulsate to the rhythm of vina strings
Pulled tense to pitch between round gourds,
Resounding still though no longer strummed,
And of long cylindrical drums

With skin stretched tight and tied with thongs
That rest upon the loins of squatting drummer.
Cymbals of bronze, once struck together,
Vibrate in the hand and sing.

Above them on the wall an ecstatic dancer pauses,
Standing on one bent leg turned outward
And holding the other flexed and suspended.
Her breasts, her belly throb,
Her torso arches right with arm flung high,
Her head slants toward her left shoulder
With blissful eyes gazing obliquely downward.
The pendent flower bud upon her armlet trembles,
Her girdle's braided tassel sways between her thighs.

Higher, the back of a woman in bright relief,
Left leg extended and right leg lax,
With strands of jewels hanging on dangling loops
Against a dhoti pleated tight on tilted buttocks.
Her trunk rotates and her full breast projects
Beneath her armpit as she reaches to adjust
A stud of twisted gold dropping from a chain
That follows the parting of her sinuous hair.
She glances from her niche with crescent eyes.

Higher still, a couple embraces.
Her arm encircles his neck,
And coils of her sculptured hair touch her spine
As she looks up into his face.
Her breasts are pressed
Against the sandstone pores of his chest
Below his hammered metal necklace and his flat nipples.
His head is inclined forward with eyes closed.
His arm, banded with fluted brass at the bicep
And a beaded bracelet at the wrist, reaches down,
His hand on the calf of her rising leg.

I return as I had come,
To the strip of shadow beside an isolated tree,
And peer through drifting steam and white sunlight.
The temple shifts its weight to the other hip.

SONGH

All male Sikhs are named Singh,
Which is a singularly brotherly thing.
The Sikhs like to gather in throngs
To sing their favorite old Singh songs.
Either singly or in a fervent gang
They sing the songs their fathers sang.
The songs they sing are sanguine songs,
Praising right and damning wrongs.
In the world today many a mother tongue
Has unsung heroes, old and young,
But when the Sikhs' songs have been flung,
A hero Singh becomes a hero Sungh.

BALLOON-SELLERS
   Ludhiana, Punjab

Soon after dawn the balloon-sellers venture out
From the settlement of mud huts that squat
On the sloping enbankment of the Jagroan Bridge.
Wrapped in cloth grayly transparent with age,
A young girl, a boy, three men go off singly,
Black hair tangled and dark eyes dulled,
Carrying their green and pink and gold balloons
Tied to bamboo poles that rest against their shoulders.
Their bare feet imprint their fragile human mark
Upon the wide truck tracks and the interwinding
Serpentine impressions of a thousand cycles
In the thick dust at the sides of the roadbed.

They whose lives are heavy, sell the lightest wares,
They whose lives are drab, sell the brightest wares,
They who possess only life can sell only life--
Their breath in colored spheres of air.

THE PEACOCKS OF NARANGWAL

Surveying their Punjab of village and wheatland,
Grasping the bricks with strong golden claws,
Haughty and regal they perch on the rooftops,
The elegant peacocks of Narangwal.
As the afternoon sunlight emblazons their feathers,

They coil and then stretch out their blue necks to call,
One cock to another, from rooftop to rooftop,
May-awe, may-awe, may-awe.

In Narangwal village the peacocks are dancing,
As a breeze through the field rustles the straw,
Their tails iridescent like bright burnished metal,
They dance for their subjects, they dance to enthrall.
They circle, they rotate to every direction,
Their tail feathers quiver, then suddenly fall,
And with the sunset they fly up to their branches,
May-awe, may-awe, may-awe.

Come dance on a rooftop in Narangwal village,
In brilliant blue turban, in dazzling green shawl,
Move boldly in circles to primitive rhythm,
Now bow before one and now bow before all.
Come dance on a rooftop in Narangwal village,
Proclaim who you are from the highest brick wall.
Shout over the houses so all the world hears you,
May-awe, may-awe, may-awe.

STUDY QUESTIONS

1. Take an object, or flower, as Ray Griffith has in his
   "Roses" and try to find out everything you can about that
   object. Then try writing a poem based on your research.
   How is Griffith's poem different, but yet similar, to Angela
   Peckenpaugh's "Rose"?

2. In "Khajuraho" the poet describes *bas-relief* in sandstone.
   Find pictures of Indian architecture and see if you can't
   begin to see what Griffith experienced. Discuss how this is
   a *spatial poem*.

3. "Roses," "Dewey Decimal" and "Songh" *rhyme* in *couplets*.
   Explore with your instructor the various possibilities of
   stanza forms (*tercets, quatrains, octets*) available to a poet.
   How does each stanza form create a different effect?

4. Try to recall a special place in the city, or country, where
   you saw something unusual or uncommon. Read
   "Balloon-Sellers" and try to capture, in a short poem, a
   similar effect.

5. As something of a different exercise, ask your instructor about *scansion,* then try to *scan* "The Peacocks of Narangwal." What insights can you make about the *metrics* of this poem? What words have a heavier *accent?* Find out why this poem is "dance-like."

Arthur Madson

Born and raised and educated in Iowa. Grew up both in small town and on farm. Oldest of six. Father Danish, Mother's American ancestors go back to Dutch in New Amsterdam. Early learned a good book was far more trustworthy than a human being; hence somewhat reclusive, unpopular, and impervious to peer pressure.

Army service (stateside) and Bachelor's, Master's, wife and first two children on GI Bill. At UW-W (third teaching position) since 1960. Came late (after age 50) to writing poetry, but haven't stopped since starting. You can find me at my desk in Heide Hall most any time, writing (or reading).

In voice and vocabulary I try to render the tension of such traditional opposites as innocence and experience, youth and age, male and female, remembering and anticipating, and so on. I try to avoid the easy allure of originality and the false enticement of the bizarre. Try to orient the reader--locate the poem--in time or place or both. I never begin with a mood or emotion but with a situation, a human situation, the more humdrum the better, and try to invest the situation, as it develops, with emotion. I try to make the many concretions of the situation, if not an analogy strictly for some abstraction or philosophical attitude, at least buzz with their reverberations. I try never to forget that, though everything is a game, scoring is not necessarily the goal. Of course there are always exceptions.

COUSINS

I grew up with cousins,
older cousins, younger cousins, same-age cousins,
boy cousins, girl cousins,
blond cousins, dark cousins,
town cousins, farm cousins,
brown-eyed cousins, blue-eyed cousins, even a green-eyed,
red-haired cousin,
tall cousins, short cousins, skinny cousins,
two or three chubby cousins,
fair cousins, tanned cousins,
freckled, pimpled, peach-skinned cousins,
clear-sighted cousins, four-eyed cousins,
sports-star cousins, cheering cousins, clumsy cousins,
one crippled-from-infantile-paralysis cousin,
better off cousins, and poor ones,
bike-owning, riding cousins,
bike-borrowing cousins,
Lutheran cousins, some Methodist cousins,
Baptist, and even one family
of Catholic cousins,
Madson cousins, and other cousins,
three dozens of cousins,
I grew up with cousins;
I thought everyone did.

I grew up in the same small town
my father did;
his older brother and younger sister
lived there too, just blocks away,
and thirteen kids, thirteen cousins,
allies always,
each at home
in all three houses.
Two cousins and I,
one boy, one girl,
one blond, one brown,
one Madson, one other,
like triplets, almost,
went through all eight grades,
together,
went to Sunday school,
together,
played kick-the-can, anny-I-over,

jacks and hopscotch and hide and seek,
prisoner's base, marbles, and mumbledy-peg,
together,
built snowmen and snow forts,
sledded and skated and giggled and teased
and did homework,
together.

All the cousins were small-town kids
or farm kids,
and none lived far away,
a half or one or two hour trip,
at most;
and hardly a Sunday went by
we didn't load up and visit
one of the relatives,
or an aunt and an uncle and cousins
would come to visit us.
None of the uncles was a golfer;
all fished,
and were given to tall tales
and talk of politics
and hard times;
none a drunkard,
but all moderate drinkers of beer,
and great Sunday feasters
at summer picnics on the lawn or in the park,
at winter dinners of
meat loaf, with home-made chili sauce,
muffins and butter, real butter,
creamed cauliflower, carrots, home-crocked sauerkraut,
baked potatoes, mashed on the plate and eaten, skins and all,
or roast pork and mashed potatoes and pork gravy,
pickled apples held by the stem and nibbled all around,
spiced whole peaches, cottage cheese,
apple pie a la mode,
and cups and cups of coffee
for the adults
and older cousins
around leaf-extended dining tables.

Younger cousins at card tables
had great fun
tangling feet, bumping elbows, making faces,
gabbing and grabbing and eating

only what
and as little or as much
as we chose, free from
adult advice
as long as we got along--
so we did, but teetered with care on the edge.
The older among us
enjoyed our rank,
pseudo adults,
and grieved and hankered for
graduation from Kool-Aid and wiggly card table
to coffee and grown-up dining.

Parents and aunts and uncles often spoke
of their cousins,
and of the children of those cousins,
cousins once removed,
our second cousins--
we knew the terms--
and spoke to us darkly of cousin's marrying,
warning of genetic danger in such consanguinity,
citing cousins who had married anyway,
hinting of passion, rebellion, Eden's apple,
and whose children all, sure enough,
paid the price--
examples, or exceptions, every one.

All the cousins spoke of
our other cousins,
cousins on the other side,
unrelated cousins complicating
relativity,
yet when we sometimes met these cousins' cousins,
our visits overlapping,
we felt an instant twinge of kinship, cousinhood.
In the family trees we'd climbed and combed
we'd found cousins twice or more removed,
and cousins of third or fourth or more degrees,
in the hundreds,
so that sometimes, citing Genesis, we claimed
all the world as cousins.

Each family, my mother's and my father's,
gathered for a family picnic
every June and August--

sacred family holidays.
All the aunts and uncles
and the cousins
always came,
even the Catholic ones,
skipping Mass that Sunday,
and always a family or two
of some distant cousins
we'd never seen before, but knew--from family gossip--
and always they turned out to be
blond, brown, stingy, nice,
formal, casual, stuck-up, friendly,
just like all the closer cousins,
and had familiar names.

Cousins chose up sides for volleyball
and softball, remembering each one's skills,
jumped rope, pitched horseshoes, played "Old Maid,"
and "Authors,"
and talked and walked and flirted--
one can have an awful crush
on a slightly older cousin--
and ate.
Fried chicken, ham, and fish--
pickerels, catfish, croppies, bass--
pans and pans of baked beans,
Waldorf salad, potato salad, tossed salad,
deviled eggs, home-made breads,
jams and jellies and honey,
sweet corn, cucumbers,
creamed new potatoes parsley sprigged,
sliced tomatoes and iced tea,
pies and cakes and red, ripe melon--
oh, the spitting of seeds
and dripping chins--
every June I stuffed myself
on olives my mother's sisters brought.

> That was years and years ago,
> more than I care to count,
> growing up before the war,
> and I don't correspond
> with any of the cousins;
> we've scattered from coast to coast.
> My sister stays in touch,

and her letters each contain
a chorus of tidings of cousins.
"Della's Eileen has had her first,
Della and Harold's fourth
grandchild;
Jerry retired in June,
and he and Rhoda have moved
to California.
They found a cancer, thank God, in time,
in Myrna, she had a breast removed
(which one, I wonder, seeing a slim,
blond, teen-aged
Myrna
in a red swim suit).
Poor Ralph, laid off last spring,
lost his pension;
they're living on what Karen makes
at Mrs. Paul's, she's on the line,
hopes she can hang on two more years,
till Social Security."
Cousins' children seem to graduate
by the score,
and marry and divorce,
change jobs, move about,
give birth, get sick and well, constantly.
Each item I'm grateful for,
whether news be bad or good;
each starts a flow of memories
of early times, static times,
lilac times--
times lost, times over,
preserved in ragged snapshot albums,
sauce for revery.

The war scattered the cousins,
killed one, shot up another,
but we all left, even those few who stayed behind,
left our cousin times,
and the years after
were no return;
no one came really back.
The post-war years, getting started years,
were years of losing track.

My children barely know their cousins,
let alone mine,
have grown up deprived
of cousins,
though, never having known
what they've missed,
they don't think it much;
see nothing amiss
in our family's
singularity,
and think me odd
when I reminisce--
"That's Dad."
My children barely know their cousins,

don't attend their weddings,
nor the funerals
of my aunts and uncles,
though I do,
memories winding down,
mostly done;

and though there's always smiles and hugs
and cousin's kissing,
and friendly handshakes,
there's not much to say;
ghosts from family picnics,
younger selves,
crowd the pews,
enclose the graves,
drooping their heads,
dropping their purple sprigs,
telling over and over,
loss, loss.
I grew up with cozenage;
every grown-up does.

THE BOOJUM TREE

is a ghostly, turnip-white,
twenty-foot desert shrub
of the family Fouquieraceae,
spreading spiky, broomstick branches
and disappearing in Mojavi haze,

if haze there ever be,
a deracinated root,
standing on its meditative head,
absent-mindedly exposing itself,
dreaming diurnally,
or a scarecrow, robbed of clothes and face,
scaring where no crows ever be,

or a single strange tusk,
relic of the Great Snark,
upright, bleaching in the sand,
growing miraculously
a waxy desert bloom
that disappears overnight,

or Georgia O'Keefe's picture
reproduced botanically--
stark head bone and tan silence
locked in fatal dalliance,
if rooted shrub the dance of death can be.

With silent tongue the tree speaks
of artists, poets, snarks
defying temporality.
It tells of forests where
no forests really be.

SHE HAWK

Sharp-shinned death struck the dove
in our backyard on Friday, and maybe
thought our feeder was his hawk's
trove and privilege, because he
struck twice more before
his long weekend was done.

We never saw him strike the doves,
just heard their awful coo.
Barely larger than his prey,
with longer, stiffer tail and wings,
he ripped and gorged, while we
swallowed behind the pane.

For half an hour or so he devoured
his spoil, digging, tugging, gulping,
sprinkling blood, as we gaped at the

carnival, and leaving, at last, inside
the feathered clump, just shards
of bones, a beak, and claws,

and round-about, crimson-spotted
snow. Rising to perch in the over-
arching maple tree, he lordly
cleaned his beak, flexed his
wings and glared at us, huddled
at the window, and arrowed

out of sight. Eileen, unbending,
praised the bird's superb
economy, pardoned the raptor
cruelty--"Hawks hawks must be,"
and swooped on me with
"too fierce to be a he."

HEIGHT REPORT

I climbed
before I walked,
Mother always said,
creeping up the stairs,
and later, scaled the banisters
and the upright piano
till she banished me.

Schoolyard swing sets and slides
existed for climbing
and shade trees everywhere
for shinnying up.
Finally reaching a handhold branch
on stubborn trunks
and hooking a leg above my head
and swinging up,
I savored the sweet
of performance and victory.

Now and then I took a fall.
Once, landing on a root,
I thought I'd gone blind,
seeing only a blur of red,
but it was just blood
from a forehead cut.

I learned to relish risk
and taking care.

Dad appointed me, age ten,
official windmill greaser,
and twice as often as really called for,
I climbed to the narrow platform,
clung to the wheel and claimed the mountain top,
peered from the crow's nest
and hallooed "Land Ho!"
and clambered down.

In high school days I climbed
the town's water tower.
Near the top the iron ladder
angled outward,
and the climber had to hang
at forty degrees
for eight or ten rungs
before gaining the catwalk,
a dangling danger I felt in the biceps,
insteps, and in the mouth.

I could see the whole town
and miles of countryside
and little people on the ground--
but the climbing itself was the point.
Only sometimes was it showing off;
more often I climbed alone,
slowly, each step a joy of movement
at once controlled, and free.

But one day, half way up the windmill,
I froze, dropped the pail of grease,
needing both hands, now, for clinging.
Two months past sixteen,
and my climbing days were done.

Well, I'd lost those heights,
but, firmly fixed on the ground,
I spoke to the girls
who admired my climbs.
I masked my flight,
salved my ache,
preferring to stroll with them, now,
on the level, on the walks.

Over the years I've gotten worse--
turn green in elevators that whoosh,
on bridges fight the urge to jump,
get dizzy on any sightseeing peak,
stand carefully back from parapet's edge,
the overlook's drop.

But I no longer really care.
My Midwest landscape,
levelled since sixteen,
is slopes and curves
whose risks and sweets
are even more savory
than the crow's nest.

BASIC TRAINING

I grew up scraping shit off my shoes--
foot in cow shit as I milked the beasts,
wading in chicken shit as I gathered the eggs,
kicking horse shit as I harnessed the team,
shod-foot, choring boy.

I scooped and emptied, every day,
the brimming gutter behind the cows;
chicken house, horse stalls, calf pens
I moved to barnyard piles of shit,
shirt-sleeved, barn-schooled youth.

I grew up taking shit. Every March
and August, I forked enormous loads
of fragrant shit aboard the shit
spreader, and drove across the fields,
sun-tanned fertilizer.

When I, careless, drove too fast,
or the wind blew wrong,
I was clodded with shit, and slowed,
or sometimes merely hunched,
speedster, growing up.

It was hard, coming in, cleaning up,
after a ten-hour work day,
and going on a Saturday date.
I'd sit in the darkened movie,
playing footsie with Darlene,

watching Gable kiss Harlow, Lombard,
Colbert, watching Bogart acting tough,
and me, shitless seventeen.

DINOSAURS

I saw dinosaurs the other day,
lumbering, mesozoic creatures, cursorial whales,
awesome carnivores espying scaly lizard prey,
nodding left and striking right with horrid, lethal tails,
dragon bipeds walking tall across the spongy lands,
carefully balanced gait on eight fantastic claws,
scratching, swatting, dangling tiny arms and hands,
standing, stuffing dripping mouthfuls down their gaping jaws,
bobbing fearsome heads with each deliberate footfall,
croaking like a swamp of frogs amorously antiphonal,
tyrannosaurus rex.

I saw the stylish dinosaurs,
vast, cretaceous brutes, log-legged leviathans,
herbivores acruise in pre-historic corridors,
reaching high for ten-yard arborescent fronds,
bog-walking behemoths, scooping floating water plants,
belly deep in tepid wallows, poikilothermous,
ponderous leaders in that aboriginal time and dance,
two-step, four-step, called the carboniferous,
long necks amove in graceful arcs, up, over, down,
pasted grins on lipless mouths, late Jurassic clowns,
balmy brontosaurus.

I saw dinosaurs of every kind,
massive, upright walkers snoring now in forest glade,
bulky bottom-walkers by a muddy bank reclined,
ugly gliding flyers perched asleep and unafraid,
a fallow, posed tableau, extinct saurian spring tide.
I even smelled the scene, stagnant, coprophilious,
till suddenly the beasts were gone, a dinosauricide.
Did the god of beasts, docently magnanimous,
because their hundred million years of reign was done,
just discard the pack, his game of solitaire lost--or won--
and deal the mammals in?

MUSICAL

Summer still, but seventh grade
looming, just a week away, tingling
all over and numb, too, numb and
dumb--I wanted to sing, and would have,
but teachers since the second grade,
and Dad had told me I couldn't--
a tin ear--but I began to suspect
the body could sing, when Pat Smith,
one of the first girls in the class
to wear a brassiere, let me touch her,
there, and leaned her shoulder into mine,
letting me know I could do it again,
so of course I did. Up on the screen
the heart-throb singer crooned, and all
the saddle shoes in the front rows screamed,
and we kissed, smashing our lips until I
lost my balance, slipped, and knocked her
glasses off. We were shy awhile, pretending
to watch the screen, and then I slid my
whole hand over her breast, and she touched
me where I was, inside my clothes, as hard
as the seat arm. The movie ended, the
lights came on, the organ played, and all
the kids began to climb up the aisles.
We stood and bumped along the row and
stumbled toward the lobby, unready for
the descent to bright lights and afternoon
chitchat. Out on the sidewalk we fit
our sweating palms together, holding on
as if we were drowning, and walked to Stensrud's
drugstore where we sat across from each other,
smiling, never unbuttoned, dazed and different,
singing a silent duet.

THE MYTH OF ETERNAL RETURN

For a month the grackles have plowed the garden,
turning the sodden leaves I mulched last fall,
their bills shiny colters and shares.
They always come in flocks, eight or ten
or twenty. Only in winter

70

is there ever a single grackle,
and he's broken-winged, and you know
he'll never see the spring.
They arrive mid-March, when the deepest
drift of snow is almost gone, and pose,
glossy black and heads of iridescent
green and blue, against the dirty white,
drinking from the melting edge.
They walk, they squawk, they furrow
the mulch, then startle and fly
in unison, so many black duplicates.
Predators of bug and slug and grub,
they never hunt alone, like the hawk
or owl, but plow the field in gangs.
They are a school; they conform, like geese
in skein, like larks in exaltation.
There a male ruffs his feathers, points
his beak, and treads so grossly
that Anne and I, behind the pane,
laugh and turn to each other--grackles
in tandem, moldboards in springtime.

STUDY QUESTIONS

1. After reading Arthur Madson's "Cousins," try to think of all
    your relatives. Compose a "family history" much as the poet
    has. This is one of the longest poems of the collection.
    What gives the poem its momentum? What keeps you reading
    all of it?

2. Look up all the words you are unfamiliar with in "The
    Boojum Tree" and "Dinosaurs." Once you are aware of these
    words and terms, discuss how these words are appropriate
    for each poem. How does *vocabulary* enrich each poem?

3. Re-cast "Height Report" from first person singular to
    second, and then third person singular. How has the poem's
    tone changed? Discuss the *informal tone* of this poem. What
    are the advantages of each choice of pronoun?

4. "Basic Training" challenges your assumption about what is, and isn't, an appropriate subject for poetry. How has the poet used *humor* to counter an otherwise disgusting subject?

5. After reading "The Myth of Eternal Return," try to explain, in a short essay, why this is a poem. Include a discussion of the long *stanza* (what purpose?), *poetic language, (personification, metaphor, repetition)* and *imagery*. How does the poem address the comment by the American poet, William Carlos Williams, "no ideas but in things"?

Andrea Musher

I am a transplanted East Coast native, having grown up just outside Washington D.C. and completed my undergraduate degree at Cornell University in Ithaca, New York. Although I flirted briefly with palm trees, ocean sunsets and smoggy freeways for a year in L.A., for the past dozen years or so I've lived in and around Madison, Wisconsin accepting the seasoning influences of cornfields and frigid wind chill temperatures. I've supported my habit of writing poetry with a variety of paying jobs including making omelettes, acting in dinner theater, teaching, and helping to establish a postsecondary education program in two state prisons.

Why do I write poetry?

--Because everything else is work.

Everything else is something I *should* write, ought to finish.

Poetry is spontaneous conversation with myself.
It comes or it doesn't.

It's about joy and discovery (even when it's about great
  pain and sorrow)
It's a new way of knowing what I don't know.

Poetry's grace and time alone.
A way of understanding experience more deeply, a way of
  experiencing the fusion of thought and feeling, image
  and idea

I write poetry because I like giving poetry readings.
And the people who care about poetry generally care about
  other things that are important to care about.

Because we are all broken and in need of healing.

Because words are magic.

Because what we write down lives longer than us, and it's
  nice when more than laundry lists and the counting of
  how many sheaves of grain are owed to the king,
  survive us and the people we chose to love.

THE FATHER

He had three daughters
lovely as a china teaset
their feathery fine hair clipped close
along the base of their skulls
and above their ears

He woke them nights
beating his brass bell
for firedrills
and they ran into the cold
wet towels around their bare necks
like a strangler's embrace

They dreamed of long hair
curled/braided
hanging from trees
and towers
beaded with birds
and twined with seaweed

He dreamed of his three daughters
his three silver teaspoons
he longed to carry in a chamois pouch
always at his waist
and their hair grew before him
in wings of flame

So he would rise each morning
stalking them with his silver scissors
snipping the air
in a fury of love

IN BOTSWANA

where they live
have always lived
it's dry and deep inland
they know dust
a few hens scratching behind the huts
stalks of corn
whose swelling green sheaths
they watch anxiously
they know the money their parents paid
for school fees

the idea of the sea
water so big you can't see
land on the other side
is stranger to them
than the notion of infinity
You are teaching
Hemingway's "The Old Man and the Sea"
because it's on the required reading list
and they have no mind pictures
for ships and masts
for waves and tide and surf
though they sit respectfully
sometimes three skinny ones to one chair
because there are not enough desks
and not enough food
because the drought is almost constant
they see swirls of dust
and cannot see the waves rise and break
wet with longing

their mouths have been fed on tale-telling
the sea might as well be a god-place
from the beginning of time
that has now left the earth
they want to believe this myth called ocean
it is a good dream
a good omen, a good tale
that the white people tell

ON THE EDGE OF THE DESERT

I sit encamped
a fringe of striped canopy overhead
supported on four thin stakes
And the caravan men who pass
have loved me
There is one clay water-jug
I have always had with me
its lips to my lips
pass the secret
of moisture
in this dry wind

Long ago I wove my wedding rug
sat dazed at the loom
while birds and flowers and magic beasts
leapt from my fingers
and fastened themselves into the pattern

My marriage charm
the gift I brought
and carried from camp to camp
again again
the tent the rug and love gritted with sand

I sit on my rug alone
at the edge of a desert
a green oasis glimmers
woman/wife/widow
Now I wed myself
this the true marriage
performed most often in pain

Bone marries bone
even where the joints flame in aging
Body and brain wed by messages slowing
flowing between them
All my cells honeycombed with memories
the crowd that gathers sticky and dense
to bear witness

I am an old woman
I sit on beautiful rug
on the edge of the desert
I give my moisture
to the wind
and leather-willed
I lay down
deep roots
growing towards death

MY FAMILY

They fold their lips over the past muttering
"Leave well enough alone"
No fondness for old photos
Mute brown eyes bring
too much death

77

My parents have lived
all these salt and sweet years
without their parents
And the Camps of World War II
swallow the horizon
like a subway tunnel
that contains every journey home

I long for a circle of stories
to see my grandparents arriving at Ellis Island
to see a kerchiefed grandmother holding
a baby on her hip while stirring soup
making mandelbrot and arguing politics

Where's Amalia
my mother's mother for whom I was named
she of the perfect pastry and fading recipe book
Where's Grandma Rebecca
of the magnifying reading glass and Yiddish newspaper
the bootlegger who supported the family
And my father says:
"Sha! Dont' tell Andrea about the bootlegging.
She'll write about it"

MESSAGES BETWEEN US

for Valentine's Day
your first without Dad
I sent Narcissus
spirit flowers in white ruffs
reaching from their bowl of stones
in the heart of the cold
and oh mother you tell me I have sent you
the ghost of your mother
who planted narcissus bulbs
in a special bowl every fall
how as a child you waited by the winter window
(I see you there in your long curls and hair ribbons)
for the thin stems to unfurl
their fragile veined scarves
a promise of something that hurt and healed
as the season dull and dirty
ground down the streets
and tattered snow froze and thawed

they say Narcissus gazed at himself too long
as you look at these reflecting flowers
your mother dead for thirty years
walks the house you built without her
one day she was feeding your first child
the next day she was dead
she who had brushed your hair
made your clothes planned your
days loved your friends arranged
your marriage and fed you
the music that sang in her
took the tasks from your hands
and placed you before the piano
and it was enough for her that
the keys under your fingers
wove passion scarves
that danced her soul clean
of the tedium and despair she would never accept
as partners
        one day her love was a walled garden
        holding you heavy with fragrance
        balmy with leaf and root
        rich with shade and wind-gentling trees
        pungent with herb-smell and promise
the next day she was dead
and your stomach turned and churned
gnawed inward bleeding and scarring
scar tissue growing on scar tissue
the ulcers your memories raging within
you shut it away
knowledge of this life without her
named me for her
and willed me close
so that we still live in one thin skin

You look at the flowers I have sent
and cry into a long distance
telephone call: Everyone is dying

I know each death brings the others
and I want to say
it's all right
welcome your dead home
they live and love you
even now
sending messages
between us

79

AT THE STOUGHTON COUNTY
JUNIOR FAIR: THE PIG JUDGING

Now I'm really rooting
we sit in the mini-bleachers
on the open side of the barn
they are judging the barrows
--medium sized porkers

Behind us, the sheep in their pens
some black-faced and strong
some fluffy wobbles of white
ma-ah-ah-ing

My mother is beside me
the other mothers gage
their children's chances
the smell of manure
the heat the heat
they must judge quickly
the animals are suffering so

The children lead their pigs around the ring
with small whips and canes
the rule: never come between
your pig and the judge

"This pig was past its prime 2 weeks ago"
"I like a pig that gets off its front legs properly"
a proper pig trot
no waddling
and watch for the right amount of flesh
over the shoulder bone

I dream up talent acts for them
one has volunteered to climb
the highest silo in the state
another has designed a quilt
featuring famous pigs in american history
one plays expert tennis
but has consistently failed the hormone test
for the pro circuit

the pigs pass by in review
the ribbons are being awarded
the winners go round again
they are rich in grease
and moon-meat
the cleaver at the end
will sever
a pride as redolent as ours

REDEMPTIVE POWERS

On the radio call-in talk show
the elderly woman gardener heard
that the Chinese cook with
three thousand different vegetables

For days she made lists of every
legume and tuber, vine and
stalk she'd ever raised
in forty-five years of seed and sweat
Then every vegetable she'd
ever bought or used
any root or pod she'd ever heard of
And the list was not even in the
hundreds let alone the thousands
How could her vegetable vocabulary
be so limited?
Her fancied encyclopedic knowledge was
a scant handful of index cards
that did not put down tendrils
in the dark soil of imagination's
infinite variety of forms

She dreamed of tomatoes
crossed with asparagus
of artichokes ringing
in church belfries
of parsnips and rutabagas
in decorator colors
eye-charts bearing
the symbols of edible ferns
of teas and soups that had
umbilical cords still pulsing in the ground

She dreamed of the intimate embrace
of vegetable lovers
and the Wise Hermit Vegetable
hidden somewhere in his mountain grotto
reciting his mantra that contained
the sound of the names of all of his
brethren in the universe
and whose presence healed the lame of hope

So that waking she knew
she must set forth on a sacred pilgrimage
paying homage to the grasses
of the roadside ditches
the weeds that even now were revealing
their nutritive values to the initiates
who wandered forth among them

There were thorns to be gathered
cuttings to be transplanted
bulbs to be stored
as a god-force green within her
compelled her in her labors

Though on the horizon
a cloud of bombs brewed
a bitter harvest
still the earth whispered:

>   I am with seed

>   I am with seed

WHEN THE LIGHT IS GOOD

In the film the guerrillas come to the village
and they say:

>   We know you
>   We too use claypots and machetes

Almost everyday the villagers find more
dead bodies thrown by the roadsides
fingernails have been pulled loose
ears have been cut off
cigarette scorchmarks are distinguishable

Many villagers have taken to the mountains
to escape the army raids
exiled in their own country
they share what little food and shelter
can be devised

The camera films on days when
the light is good
the weather mild
We see beautiful brown-skinned people
wearing bright hand-embroidered clothing
mothers with glossy thick black braids
breastfeeding babies wrapped in
handwoven colorful shawls
Some faces have hollows
where teeth have fallen out
But all the scenes glow
image a tantalizing rustic simplicity
though we know many die of malnutrition, exposure
have worms, lice, running sores
We do not see this
We see a clay pot
dipped in a clear mountain stream

The guerrillas living in the mountains
are young boys and young girls who have been trained
to use guns
They embroider between battles
In the cities hundreds of people pick through garbage
A woman wipes off used styrofoam plates

The camera always frames the Generalissimo
in a seated close-up
a white face, white hair and dark glasses
unbreakable plastic shields
almost fill the screen
But a guard stands behind
we see only his crotch
his gun seems to grow
out of the Generalissimo's head
--the only idea

The movie is blatant propaganda
Still we remember it is a luxury
to worry about staying aerobicly fit
and repainting the kitchen

a luxury to think of failure
as anything other
than causing pain, real destruction
The movie ran late
Survival is a question
It's time to go home
Shall we dream of a night sky
that lets the scattered fragments
of our lives shine
like clearly patterned constellations
Shall we remember this half-moon lolling lopsided?
--it's a sky cradle   a lover's cheek

AN APOCRYPHAL INTERVIEW
  (with Georgia O'Keefe)

The lines in her face were the energy
gathered
from looking
into the light

>The hills stitch their seams of color behind my eyes
>and I go on painting
>the wind grit of the dry roads I travel
>hones me finer
>
>in Wisconsin I remember the high grass beyond the barn
>needling up under my pinafore
>and the cowbells telling time for the town
>the corn rows were an unknown jungle
>I wove into being
>I tied colored rags to a whole row of stalks
>pennants licking the thick July air like flames
>
>I loved the small Texas towns of the '20's
>only a rusting auto against the lurid sunset
>so much empty land spread like a bolt of calico
>on the countertop of the dusty general store
>
>in New York all the ladies wore hats
>with small veils and delicate kid gloves
>I couldn't find gloves large enough for my hands
>and I looked ridiculous in hats
>At the gallery opening I wore men's work gloves

people asked if I was trying to make "a statement"
I told them to forget about me
and look at the paintings

I am a juggler
tossing and balancing the close of day
the hum of soft color diminishing over the water
and the moon so close
a drumskin of vibrating light
lifting my breasts and my breath

This may be the last year of my life
No, there's nothing I would do differently
I've always painted
what I could see

IN BLACK EARTH, WISCONSIN

thistles take the hillside
a purple glory of furred spears
a fierce army of spikey weeds
we climb through them
your mother, two of her daughters, and me
a late walk in the long June night

in the barn the heart throb
of the milking machine continues
as your father and brother change
the iodide dipped tubes
from one udder to the next
and the milk courses through the pipeline
to the cooling vat
where it swirls like a lost sea in a silver box

we are climbing to the grove of white birch trees
whose papery bark will shed
the heart-ringed initials of your sister
in another year
as the grief wears down

this farm bears hay and milk
and this mother woman walking with us
has borne nine children
and one magic one is dead:

                    riding her bike
                    she was a glare of light
                    on the windshield of the car
                    that killed her

a year and a half has passed
and death is folded in among the dishtowels
hangs in the hall closet by the family photos
and like a ring of fine mist around the dinner table

we stand on a hill looking at birch bark
and poking among hundred year old graves
that have fallen into the grass
rubbing the moss off and feeling for the names
that the stone sheds
we are absorbing death like nitrates
fertilizing our growth

this can happen:
                    a glare of light
                    and an empty place
                    wordlessly we finger her absence
already there are four grandchildren
the family grows thick as thistle

SNOW AND ASHES

It's a white-out
Earth and sky sink
into seamlessness
Thick wet wisdom
clamps down on the world
as distances disappear
Road signs are swaddled and mute
and there's no center-line
to divide or guide
only now and again the dim pearls
of oncoming headlights
suggest there is another
direction to travel in
and that believing in the road's continuance
or the existence of a destination
has always been a matter of faith

Sometimes the scrabble of cornstalks
barn roofs and house frames
emerge into a moment's definition
behind a windscreen
shielding my view
I shake my head
trying to clear my vision
as fragments of white
fly at me
and at me

The world is torn paper
snow and ashes
memories gone out of focus
no way to solidify live words
on pages that are being erased
as we go

But I say to myself:

> Those fir trees
> have dark-boned wings
> under the white weight of snow
> that girds them to ground

THE FITTING

I sit spread
fingering my vagina
learning the terrain by touch
feeling for my cervix

> (our skin is tucked in
> like hospital corners
> like a red mitten
> full of baby teeth and snowflakes
> like a sweater turned inside out
> so the initials won't show)

I hold the round hand mirror
and the speculum's tongue of light
touches the red eye
the sperm mustn't thread
I memorize my features
only available by reflection

Once again a woman asking a mirror
for knowledge of herself
I imagine an exam:
Choose your own from the ten below--

Now the nurse has taken my measure
the spring on this thing
is vicious
and will snap back at me
sooner than slide into place
I am setting a trap
I may catch myself
in the act

STUDY QUESTIONS

1. In the poem "My Family," why won't the poet's family talk to her about the past? Why are the last lines of the poem somewhat *ironic?* What are some of the "old stories" of the past that intrigue you that your family talks about or doesn't talk about?

2. Up until its conclusion, "At the Stoughton County Junior Fair: The Pig Judging" seems to be a humorous spoof. What's the joke? What is the "pig judging" being compared to? Taking the ending into account, why do you think the poet uses this *implicit analogy?*

3. "In Black Earth, Wisconsin" is one of several "farm landscape" poems in this collection. Re-read Ron Ellis' "Scenes of Green Light," "Addition," and "Preserves," Arthur Madson's "Basic Training" and compare, as well as note the differences, to Andrea Musher's poem. What do all three poets have as a focus? What values and attitudes are expressed? For those of your with farm backgrounds, how realistic are these poems? For those of you raised in urban environments, how realistic are these poems?

4. "Snow and Ashes" mirrors the experience of driving through a blizzard. What happens to the *speaker's vision* as she continues driving? Why do you think the poet used the word "ashes" in the title? Can you point to specific lines that suggest the poem is about something more than just a heavy snowstorm?

5. Does the opening *stanza* of "The Fitting" surprise you? At what point did you realize the woman in the poem is being fitted for a diaphragm? Do you find the poem shocking? Amusing? Intriguing? Explain why. In a class discussion, try to explore the way in which "The Fitting" challenges your values as to what is and isn't appropriate poetic material.

Angela
Peckenpaugh

Angela Peckenpaugh was born in Richmond, Virginia in 1942 and grew up in Charleston, West Virginia and Kensington, Maryland. She moved to Milwaukee in 1968 where she taught literature and creative writing at U.W. Milwaukee, Milwaukee Institute of Art and Design, and U.W. Extension. She joined the U.S. Whitewater faculty in 1982 after appearing as a guest at the Friends of Poetry Festival. Her books of poetry include: *Letters from Lee's Army,* Morgan Press; *Discovering the Mandala,* Lakes & Prairies Press; and *A Book of Charms,* Barnwood press. Forthcoming from Artist Bookworks of Chicago is *A Heathen Herbal.* Ms. Peckenpaugh is also a color xerox artist and publishes poem notecards through Sackbut Press.

I began writing poetry and reviews of poetry around 1972. My mentors were Anne Sexton, Adrienne Rich, Tom Montag and Steve Lewis. I wrote for self expression and in response to the political climate of the women's movement. I had been a teacher of composition and modern American & British Literature but began in the early 70's to teach primarily literature by women, particularly contemporary women. My life was informed by theirs and consequently I wanted to pass on my own experiences and insights in the wake of the deaths of my parents and a divorce, a growing sense of independence and purpose.

My first book explored my southern, maternal roots. The next, *Discovering the Mandala,* marked an arrival at a substiture for my lapsed Episcopalian faith. The mandala appears often in this book as a symbol for the whole self, the union of opposites, the cycles in nature. By the time I wrote *The Book of Charms* I considered myself a pagan, part of a trend among women who identified with the Old Religion of the first healers and nature worshippers rather than a patriarchal based spirituality. I adopted the persona of a witch in this book as a vehicle to use poetry in a shaman-like way to exorcise depressive and counterproductive mind states and arrive at a positive and synchronistic stance to the future.

The reading for the charm book led to *The Heathen Herbal,* an appreciation for plants and their lore, as well as their culinary and medicinal properties. Researching this book, I was led to knowledge of Druidic and Celtic narratives which I employed in my fairy tale rewrites where I hoped to present such archetypes as fairies, witches and stepmothers in a more favorable light.

For the past year I have been re-examining the meaning of love and writing a "garden variety" of love poems. Some of my current literary "heros" are Wendell Berry, May Sarton, Sharon Olds, Starhawk, Gwendolyn Brooks and Emily Dickinson. I like the whole give and take of the life of writers and artists: the rituals and celebrations, the collaborations, the commingling, the stimulation, the editing, the attempt to touch and portray deep rhythms of nature as well as the responsibility to shape the community and world consciousness for the better. Though my independence and dedication to this end have not come without pain and sorrow, the rewards and satisfaction, and, yes, love, have been immense.

SNOW WHITE

This is the story
of a girl you think you know
whose cheeks were red
as her mother's blood
and whose sleep
was like the lasting snow.
Her mother died not long
after birthing her
as some flowers do
when they've borne their seed.
And her father
in his innocence, married another,
a vain queen.
As soon as the girl
had grown to loveliness
this queen was
afraid she'd prove a distress.
You see, she insisted
on being the fairest
in the land, and
strove to have the girl slain,
but not by her own hand.
For this, she chose her hunter,
a man of integrity
and when he got the girl
in the woods, of course,
he set her free.

The queen, to increase her power,
had asked for the girl's heart
and liver which she
intended to devour.
The hunter presented instead
a pig's heart and liver,
still red with blood.
The older woman had them cooked
and on them she fed.

Now to the mirror she went
to ask if she'd improved.
The mirror, quite truthful,
didn't say what she'd hoped.
In anger, she knew she'd been duped.

Meanwhile, Snow White had come to a house
where 7 beds and 7 bowls
she tried. She used one of each
that seemed just right.
The owners, all dwarves,
returned from the mines
and agreed to adopt her
if she cared for their home.
The one whose bed and bowl she had
appropriated, shared with the others
so she learned to make herself of use
and grew in harmony with the little men
as a sun among planets, none impeding,
none too greedy. But the queen,
who was no stranger to vanity
appeared at the door when the dwarves were off
disguised as an old lady selling cloth.
The girl, who didn't detect the ruse
let the queen wind a big handsome scarf
tightly about her bodice.
The queen left Snow White smothered
and immobile. But the dwarves
unwound her and gave her brandy at table.
She survived, but was still not wise.
The queen reappeared in a different disguise
and gave her one from a basket of apples to try.
Its skin was red as her mother's blood,
the kind that flows monthly
and the white juicy inside
was infused like some false dreams
with a poison quite deadly.
This put Snow white
into a deathlike sleep.

But, just as you sometimes need
to dream to understand,
just as the snow must freeze
to fructify the land,
Snow White was only dormant
you can be sure. See, she had to
develope another side to her.
Til now she'd been mainly
a thing of beauty
who had learned to cook and clean
and feel some sisterly duty.

94

But she needed more sense
of purpose and craft,
thus it was right she should be
wakened by the kiss
of a future leader, a prince.
She did become his wife
and subsequently shared his life
but don't think she was just a pawn.
She'd learned that to adorn alone
can lead to dangerous insecurity.
You could say that their kingdom
was equally run, or that he was the moon
and she was the sun. One was the stem,
the other the flower, at any rate, no
one had too much power.

The step queen aged poorly
and eventually died. Snow White's father,
with new eyes, took no other bride.
His kingdom united with hers
and was known for its mines
of precious healing stones
and its flourishing farms.

FROM A LETTER BY MY GREAT GRANDFATHER, HAM CHAMBERLAYNE, VIRGINIAN, AT THE CIVIL WAR FRONT, 1862, TO SALLY GRATTAN

For who would change
our circle of seasons
bringing new beauty
with every revolving moon.

There is scarcely
a day of the whole year
fails to bring
a beauty of its own.

Contemplation of nature
gives pleasure unlike others,
pleasure wholly pure.

When passed,
leaving no sting of regret.
When present
never palling on the mind.

A strange tender melancholy
hangs about first fall days.
Some happiness some
state of being
never yet imagined fully
yearned for by instinct.

In every engagement
as the fire has grown hotter
and death in many horrid shapes
came nearer and nearer
the more vivid
have grown images of scenes
and pleasures past.
Imagined parlour scenes
and home circles strike
amidst angry buzzing
minie balls.

Fall weather has come again,
the year composing itself
to a decent death.

The nearer we are to the enemy
the greater the inclination
to jest.

GYROMANCY
  (Divination by circles)

Trees this time of year
are full of berries.
Before snow falls,
limbs are like iron filligree,
offering numinous protective
circles, amulets of yellow apples,
blue privet and holly.

After walking and collecting
berried branches, I come home
and paint wooden balls
blue, red and gold
in imitation and hang
them at windows on colored
threads to await the solstice.

They'll be bestowed
to the house tree
with straw stars, paper
snow flakes reminiscent
of that winter sight
which like white paper
isolates these cycles
that divine
like ritually lighted candles
in imitation of the sun.

TO CAPTURE THE POWER OF A DAY LILY

Tall, graceful necked like giraffes
or ballet dancers, reaching to the sun,
you lean toward the window,
some with arms wide, some secretively closed
to open at a later time.
The readiness with which you
flash your charms is enough
to take my breath away.
When your orange curves reveal
a star of saffron, small
shapely arms exposed within,
all to close tomorrow
I want to make a lasting monument
to your bravery. Such a nervy
way to live and die!
If I could reach the sun fearlessly
I would fall like you into a bright
pattern, that sways on the hill,
pleases the eye. Give me
your modest harmony
and imminent return.
I'll ornament paths
and windows to wake the others,
releasing color and vibrancy,
a willingness to offer
and be seen in time,
a sense of transient riches,
appreciation of each single dime.

FROM HIROSHIMA
by John Hersey

This was the first chance
she had to look at the ruins

The last time she had been
carried, unconscious

Even though the wreckage
had been described to her
and though she was still in pain
the sight horrified and amazed

Over everything
in gutters, along the river banks
tangled among tiles
and tin roofing
climbing tree trunks
was fresh
vivid, lush green

The verdancy rose
even from the foundations
of ruined houses

Everywhere were bluets,
goosefoot, morning glories,
day lilies,
sesame, panic grass

It seemed as if a load of seed
had been dropped with the bomb.

(Found poem)

AMARYLLIS

You came enclosed
in dirt, a green line above
the brown horizon, my
winter room. Like the year
that holds untold
ventures, you rise unprecedented.
One day a torch, the next
a wand, your moves are sensual,
more than I'd have mined.

The room becomes your chamber
I intuit rocking to music
leaving the rest behind. Red
Victrola trumpets
of bold tubas pronounce
winter's antidote,
weather's artifice and pose.
Expanding color
will not let me close
that private opening,
sure step to arched repose.

THE BRIDGE THAT LEADS TO BLUE

If I could hold in these lines
the snow on crossed logs
as grey green water coursed under
I would share with you the intricate
fingers of icy flowers ascending the wall
the falls tumbled over,
that sound which from a distance
seemed the wind in stark sunned limbs,
a clean hissing that drew me
like long thin shadows
across smooth stubbled snow.

Among black sticks and red partridge berries
I headed whitely toward hemlocks,
each crunch of step
each astringent intake of breath
a strangely sexual experience.
Dark flow down curved flat stairs solaced.
At the green roofed river's edge
I told deep warm brown rocks
I have been from you too long.
My father I make peace with your watery
woodland spirit cold.
My love I will soon be home.

But only alone in this forest
far more lovely than I can tell
do I know what makes us
try to repeat that world.
I have entered the angle of bent leaves

the breath of three horses munching hay
the boards of the bridge that leads to a vision
of the wet waving hue of clear sky.

ROSE

Flower of flowers,
church windows' center,
lovers' lips kiss you
and floors are strewn
so your perfume and color will
pleasantly alter the mood.

Empress Josephine carried one
to hide her ugly mouth.
Mumtaz, mistress of the Taj
Mahal bathed each day
in the pool, that was covered
with petals the night before.

Anthony wanted to die in a room
where roses reminded him
of Cleopatra's gowns
of Cleopatra's blushing breasts.

Rose water for complexion,
roses of contemplation,
roses eaten with almonds and
ice cream, you are legend
in Texas, form designs
on dresses, a ceiling's sculpture
to make us forget lines
or secrets told under your sign.

Eros is a rose, a rose is eros
despite the Tokyo kind
and despite Gertrude Stein.
Grow erotically on my pillow
and settle my mind.

VALENTINES

Tracing the origin of shapes
I came upon that biforcated puffed up heart
and often wondered if
it took its form in imitation
of cupid's bottom or a woman's breasts.
Perhaps the tip of a penis,
a love bow stretched.

The answer is given in the history of masks.
It was the human profile that made the shape.
From earliest times the face was painted
with eyes symetrically designed
and swirls from cheek to chin.
That cleavage was the failure
to transfer side views to one surface.

The two rounds meeting
are profiles joined
which come to us in the name of love,
for women painted themselves to draw
attention, or "bad" women, they were tattooed
with the laws of their tribe--
what they mustn't do
forever dyed on their skin.

Our innocent hearts
displayed in the evening shop window
and on the desks of children
come from our first selves
when man was mask,
advertised his essence,
her love, or the face
of the animals around
split when rendered flat.

We've split from that, and still
they stare at us, numerous and red
like dried cherries on a dead branch.

CHARM OF A CHILD

When you visit my house
it welcomes you. Your laughter
is the big tip that rewards
sink and stove so they jump
to their jobs with personality.
I learn the powers of story
teller, nurse, beguiling
you with poultice for your
skinned knee.
Even when you struggle against,
you mine my energy.
I distract you by showing
off the family treasures
and things I have chosen
to relegate to history.
As mother of ceremonies,
I find secret places
behind the furniture to
hide Easter eggs, make
a new landscape when I
trim the tree.
You bring out the purist
in me who wants to teach you
to adventure in the park
not tune in cartoons.
I reluctantly share the pleasure
of minor violations of laws
and we are amused when a dowdy
woman frowns as we light a match
to set off a cap.
Perhaps you learn fear
from me as well when I
make up goblins to run
from in ecstasy
so we can elude them
together on the close bushed road.
I tell you to hoard pennies
as if they were silver
til you can buy your
own treats instead of beg.
When you put on a nightie
and let me tuck you in,

time is left on the shelf.
I remember my own little vulnerable
self when you ask for your teddies
to be guardians when I am gone
and you disappear into dreams
in the big empty room.

CHARM OF DISGUISE

The pointed gold hat
that hides my hair,
the purple mask
I wear around my eyes
allow me to walk
beside my lover as a stranger,
allow me to lie.
The gloves covering my familiar rings
and green shoes
none of my friends have ever seen
allow me to dance
anonymously like a spy.
I have hidden my mouth
behind a mustache,
my bosom within a studded vest
that shines,
my legs in stage tights
and ballooning opera pants.

I am enigmatic, mute.
They have guessed all the names
but mine.

I feel a surge of energy
as if I were a clear blue sky,
a white sail in wind
leaving that shore,
my identity, behind.

CHARM TO WIN AT POKER
for Robert

Pick a table that parallels
the tub, not one that reflects.
Play when the moon is waxing,

not crescent. Lower your lashes.
Deal off the top, but sharpen
your memory. Talk to your opponent
til he worries with his logic.
Analyze your mistakes til
they come out in the wash.
Smile whether your hand
is good or not. Up the ante
on a hunch. Don't suck in
your breath or bark suddenly
when you get a flush or straight.
When deuces are wild, increase
the stakes. Keep rivals
in your debt. Don't fall for
queens because of their sex.
Or hoard a useless ace.
Don't deal out malice or gossip.
Keep other players in stitches
and you'll pay your rent.
Pay attention to signs in hand
and forget a kibbitzer's hex.
Be mindful how he hesitates
or clears his throat.
For five card stud put on your
pin stripe suit. For blackjack
your cowboy hat. For 7 card
stud your shades. Leave losses
at the table; don't bury a heart
in cuts. Pray to gods of chance
not the Baptists'.
Use hooch to loosen up or fake.
Go home when the right hour strikes.
Don't expect to buy a plane
ticket with the take.

REVIVAL MEETING

A white tent appears
on a vacant lot
in the core like a promise,
a sweet destination toward which we speed.
Driving past and stopping at a light
we yearn like tourists

for a seat inside to hear
the black ladies in turbans and white
beat their tambourines
at the altar in front
where gold trumpets are raised
in gospel grace above the neat
combed and bowed heads.
White tuxedos, carnations in lapels
attest to more than a Saturday night lift.
They rise and clap hands;
the very tent sways as they stamp feet.

Still smiling at their spirit
we notice in the field outside
women like grey ghosts
holding hands as if in seance
with all that's gone.
The night almost covers them
in their alien mourning.
As we get the green light
I look at people waiting at the bus stop
who pay no heed, as unaware of their grief
as the righteous community
and as far from them
as you are now from me.

STUDY QUESTIONS

1. "Snow White" re-tells the well-known fairy tale. Find a copy
   of the original *Snow White* and compare it to Angela
   Peckenpaugh's. What different effects are achieved in her
   poem? Is the *tone* of her poem different? How is the *detail*
   different?

2. "To Capture the Power of a Day Lily," "Amaryllis" and
   "Rose" celebrate the form, color, history and human delight
   of flowers. Explain how these poems are more than
   descriptions. In each poem, what is the *message*, or intent,
   of the poet?

3. "From *Hiroshina* by John Hersey" is an example of *found poetry*. These are usually found in non-poetic forms (non-fiction books, newspapers, advertisements) and are then presented, often with new *line breaks.* as poems. As an experiment, search for found poems and bring them in for class discussion. Explore several ways of presenting each found document.

4. "Charm of a Child" is an *address poem*. What are the concerns of the speaker? Why does the child not answer? Who is "charmed," the speaker, or the child?

5. Explore the *point of view* in "Revival Meeting." What *details* does the *speaker* see? Explain how the "people waiting at the bus stop" are "as far from them / as you are now from me."

Dale
Ritterbusch

Dale Ritterbusch has taught at the University of Pennsylvania, the Community College of Philadelphia, Bowling Green State University and the University of Wisconsin--Whitewater. The poems contained in this anthology are primarily from the collections *Nothing to Be Afraid Of* and *Perimeters,* which was awarded a publication grant from the Ohio Arts Council.

A poem is not merely words arranged on a page in a particular way, but the effect those words have on the reader--that is to say there is all the difference in the world between a poem and poetry. Poems exist in abundance, but poetry occurs infrequently and only when a reader is variously but strongly affected by the words he has read--as Emily Dickinson suggested, a poem should make the reader so cold no fire could ever warm him. The best poems strike deep to the core of human experience, are charged with energy and excitement, intensity and passion, and they will, when read, have a compelling effect on the reader, perhaps even altering his perceptions of the world and its experience.

To write poems which create this response is a difficult thing to do--few poems possess this capability; but therein lies the excitement, the challenge. What makes the reading and writing of poetry an invigorating and compelling enterprise is finding those few poems which, when read, will take the tops of our heads off.

NOTE ON THE VIETNAM POEMS

Readers should consider that some of these poems do not directly result from the poet's own experience, but may be based upon the experiences of others.

GOOD FRIDAY

Saying nothing
All through dinner,
They sit in the restaurant
Looking down at the table
Or staring out of the window
Never looking at each other--
Only a sidelong glance
As she reaches into her purse.

She goes to the restroom,
Returns, looks as though she'll leave
With him still sitting there, staring,
Acknowledging nothing, not even his hands;
She thinks better of it, sits down,
Waits for the food that will taste
Like ash--all senses dulled
Beneath stiff reason.

One wonders, looking on,
Why anyone would stay,
Why love brings such a hateful stare;
Surely, there must be a way
To make the heart stop all this pain,
To love again, and yet
The bill is paid.

They both walk out
Beneath a closing moon
Separated by a step--
Distance immeasurable as stars or years;
Only the silence of the evening sky
Will touch her lips, will stay with her
Though this is April, and there's snow.

A MATTER OF FACT

Rainforest mist
the green greyed by distance,
haze palling the sound

The path beneath treads soft-
layers of spongy leaves,
dark branch, muted chatter
up above

The new road runs deep,
not paved, debris piled
along the way, brush
clogging the half-filled ditch

There is no pain, no smell
of corpses reeking
in the sodden air

There is the dream of flowers
perfumed, heavy, poisoned
as the scent digs deep
into the lungs

The bus spews out soft earth,
red, gouged,
in some omniscient view
like the face warned,
cautioned against
any resistance--
"You are ours," he said
"to do with as we please."

The bus swerves and sways,
downshifting for the inclined curve
and halts, slightly, shudders,
as the gears grind and the wheels
spin

There is no thought of death
as the carbines breathe fire,
as red flowers drip poison
on the darkened earth
still heavy with the rain

There is the body thrown clear,
six others bleeding in their seats,
blood sticky on the feet
of those who found them hours later,
took them to a church and lined them
out, in the shadows of that church,
where they were stripped and bathed,
soft hands washing the crimson
smears from breast and throat,
the bodies supple,
caressed as if by lovers
as the blood runs clear

If there is mourning
no one thinks it so;
it is a commonplace
among the woodsmoke,
heavy flowers, new roads,
and the rain that comes
that afternoon, splattering
the bodies clean.

BETTER DEAD THAN BORING

This morning a Huey came in
over the campus trees
descended in a cordoned off area
near the Business Administration Building--
a show for the ROTC boys,
their sorority girls:
an impressive piece of equipment
spit shined and strac,
not even a fingerprint
on the pilot's black visor
reflecting the sun--
all that attention to detail

      . . .

"Details, candidate, details!
It's the little things that'll kill you,"
the TAC officer said, over and over
like some Biblical quote . . .

Yeah, I guess so,
like a small piece of shrapnel, no bigger
than a pin that entered the chest
under the arm, that found that one small
space in a flak jacket unprotected--it took
an hour to find the wound . . .

I sleep late now, avoid as much of the day as I can,
but the *pock, pock, pock* of the blades
carving this early morning sky . . .

Elegy, mimic of heartbeat,
song that quickens the blood;
the body shivers, sweats like cold metal

. . .

Lock and load coming over the trees
gunships prepping the treeline
the first ship down, recon by fire
a squad runs off to the left, another
lies prone in the tall grass, puts out
good cover to the front, two pigs raking the trees
tracers arcing low over the brush--
a door gunner walks fire
through a hootch, abandoned, rotting,
just in case--
another ship takes fire
a couple 79 rounds lift smoke into the trees
pinpoint a mortar crew, dug in
bracketing the LZ
another ship pulls off hit in the tail
each squad taking fire
gunships in and out of the trees--
another LZ two klicks away--
the only possibility--obvious, a set up
as the other ships land, are hit by heavy fire--
Chicom 107's--Phantoms roll in at tree top level
scream by, huge cannisters tumbling
twin balls of flame, rolling orange-black smoke
trees incinerate, oxygen sucked out of bunkers
leaving behind the smell of burning oil and flesh

. . .

There's the usual bitching about
the role of the university in military affairs
but hell, for some it's the only way out--
the only way out of a trailer park
on the edge of some cornfield--either that or be
a shit kicking farmer, or work for a potato chip
factory and come home smelling like overused grease--
better to die in Lebanon or Grenada than live in Ohio . . .

I watch the ship lift into the air
drink coffee, do nothing
for the rest of the day

CANOE TRIP

I scouted the rapids
from the ridgeline above the river--
the water dark, turbid
undercutting the crumbling riverbanks
with the swollen rush
from heavy rain.

On my left was a farmer's field,
plowed under, ready for spring planting.
Looking down at the water
I didn't notice the pit
until I was almost at its edge.
It was filled with dead pigs,
a few young ones, the rest mostly fetal
with umbilical cords still attached--
dozens of them heaped over a few large, gray sheep,
a couple of rats, a muskrat
poised, swimming through all that death,
its head resting on the back of a pig.
It looked almost alive swimming there
except its eyes had been plucked by the birds.

I was upwind as I stood at the edge
watching the rain pelt down on
the small pink bodies heaped several feet high.
Edging back, I skirted around
to the left, walked down along the ridge
on the other side of the pit;
the stench gagged me, and I choked.

The dead were on the wire,
sparawled outside the perimeter,
with many more along the tree line;
a few were inside where they'd overrun
a fire team on the left.

In the sun their bodies started
to swell--parts of bodies hung
in the trees, one arm swinging
like a Mexican piñata.

We searched most of the bodies, but the smell
made nearly everyone throw up--
and two were booby trapped.
The week before one had played possum,

113

and a man was killed next morning,
when he came out to search through the dead.

The stench gagged deep in the lungs,
and the defenses were so torn up, the engineers
just came and bulldozed all those bodies
together in a pile and buried them
under a few feet of earth--
one arm and part of its hand stuck up,
almost waving good-bye,
before it too was plowed under.

I walked back, past the woodchuck
hanging in the tree--
wedged in the V of some branches--
felt the rain
stinging my eyes.

I put in maybe thirty yards downstream
from where I'd landed--
decided to take my chances
with the rocks.

INTERROGATION

It begins with a question
a demand

As an argument from authority

You take a cigarette
and pull the rough smoke into your lungs

The interrogators are patient
and wait patiently until you exhale

Their arms are folded, in front or in back;
one of them leans across the table

This is the way you had always
pictured it to be

Except,
far back beyond any recall,
something heretical--
an element of knowledge
causing a strange displacement
and the order handed down
behind black inquisitorial masks

Now
the masks are the pallid
faces of people you grew up with,
of your neighbors, some who were once your friends

They could be anyone, you assume;
they look like anyone, they pretend like anyone--
they examine your life in front of you,
turning it over and over like a strange artifact

Beyond any degree of certainty or apprehension
it is possible to add to your ignorance;
you don't know, and every question
seems a revelation--
the world becomes informational
with all the evident abstraction of a newspaper

The orbit of the earth is a lie,
the color yellow is a lie,
the cold space between words is a lie
and everything,
spilling into the stillness you don't answer,
rings true

You tell them what you do on a Saturday afternoon--
        they have pictures
you tell them your dog has been spayed--
        the veterinarian comes out of the hall
you tell them your wife and your children . . .
        she cries and cries but says nothing;
        your daughter stares at her hands

If there were a window in this room
you would look for a tree--
the tree would move as trees do
and catch currents of sun and air;
you would climb into the branches
and look out for hours--

Perhaps dreaming of a diplocaulus
devouring a Permian fish

Other worlds have spun out of time--
other lives

You tell them everything
they want to know

IN NORTHERN ONTARIO,

On the banks of a sandy lake,
An old snapping turtle basks in the sun
Far out of reach of the warm, pulsing water.
Two leeches suck on the opened flesh of his stubby neck
Making it hard for his head to retract.
I take my knife still stained with the blood
Of fish and cut them from his heavy dark green
And brown flesh--they splatter thick blood
When I smash them stone against stone.

I search for more.
His ridged triangular plates recall
The armor of a stegosaurus, the cognitive instincts
Of fifty million generations. Patiently
His black obsidian eyes follow me
As I find heaped rings of parasites,
Like a nest of baby snakes, clinging
To the leathery folds of his webbed feet.
I cut them like bloody worms, but timorously,
As I recall baiting a snapper with a stick
As a young boy, fascinated by his ancient power
To break it in two.

Primitive surgery done, the pale pink ooze
Will cure in the sun, wash clear in the lake.
I feed him entrails from fish, launch the canoe
To catch us some more.

How sweet the lakewater tastes over fallen tangled
Trees clearly seen in depths far out from shore, and yet
Some of the bass have round yellow worms, some
Almost orange, curled in the sweet translucent
Flesh throughout the caudal peduncle, between
The neural spines. I crush the ones I can find
After digging them out or burn them,
In the fire, along with the heads of pike
And sunfish--their gills still open and close,
Their eyes still follow the movements of my hand
Even as flames feed on them with their sharp teeth.

No sign of the turtle when I return--
The scarred snapper has slipped off,
His heavy shell warmed like a stone

116

In the afternoon sun--
Not even a break in the water
As far as the eye can see
Or the light can reach.

44

The first time I saw Henry Aaron bat
He hit an easy pop up
And I sat back, dejected, impatient
Waiting for his next at bat.
It seemed forever--I was only eight,
Had time only for winning,
The grand moment, heroic gesture--

It was always the last of the ninth
2 out, behind by 3, the bases loaded
3 and 2 the count--seventh game of the World Series
And I had Henry Aaron's power;
I would foul off the next, a curve low and outside
Just nicking the corner, staying alive
As the world waited, balanced on the outcome
Of the next pitch.
Always it hung across the plate,
Belt high, as my wrists broke
And the hard crack of the ball
Resounding off that bat rose above the world
Beyond the deep left center of everything.

A thousand times, hit always to the same place
Deep in the stands, the place I watched
Waiting for Aaron's next turn at the plate.

And again he was out and again--
I could not understand
How anyone that good could fail;
I could not know the best fail most the time.

The next game went the same
Until the eighth and Aaron
Took a strike--a ball--
Then swung and missed--the next
Was low--count even,
The sign shook off and
Aaron guessed it right,
Picked up the rotation of the seams,

117

Knew it as his body sprung, forearms extended,
Wrists breaking unleashing the coiled
Power in his bat,
Cleats twisting into the dirt.

Trajectory of a bullet, sharp rise
Above the plane, the fall--
He noted where it hit
And rounded first, head down,
The noise we made like the voice of God
Thundering in the great man's ears.

I didn't want the cheers to stop,
The next batter to come up to the plate
Congratulating Henry with a slap
On his outstretched hand.
I wanted him to run the bases endlessly
Never reaching home
As I struck out, as I popped up
Going from game to game
Playing far into the night,
Far into the years.

WINNING HEARTS AND MINDS

She clasps the child to her breast--
cries as her hootch burns. Her husband
fought back--lies there--upper butt stroke
so hard it broke the phenolic stock: vengeance--
a futile gesture--spitting betel juice
into the wind.

She has lost one son to the V.C., another
to an air strike: She remembers the soft rain
of dirt falling out of the sky--
sees his chest opened like a fruit,
dug open with the nails and pulled apart--
his organs glistened like a melon.

She sobs; her eyes sing hate; her child,
clutched tighter, cries above the flames.

A marine screams, "Shut the fuck up!"

A scrawny pig is shot and tossed on the flames;
rice burns, pops like a flare.

She runs, tit flapping against her chest,
falls
against the hard luck of Vietnam.

SEARCH AND DESTROY

They came out of the hootch
with their hands up--surrendered--
and we found all that rice
and a couple of weapons. They
were tagged and it all seemed so easy--
too easy, and someone started to torch
the hootch and I stopped him--something
was funny. We checked the hootch
a couple times more; I had them probe it
like we were searching for mines and
a lucky poke with a knife
got us the entrance to a tunnel.
We didn't wait for any damn
tunnel rats--we threw down
CS and smoke and maybe two hundred
yards to our right two gooks popped up
and we got 'em running across the field,
nailed 'em before they hit the trees.
We went to the other hole and popped more
gas and smoke and a fragmentation grenade
and three gooks came out coughing, tears
and red smoke pouring out of their eyes and
nose. We thought there were more
so we threw in another grenade and one of the
dinks brought down his arms, maybe he started
to sneeze with all that crap running out of his face,
maybe he had a weapon concealed, I didn't know,
so I greased him. Wasn't much else I could do.
A sudden move like that.

AFTER THE WAR

On the drive back
from wherever he travelled to,
a flock of birds, possibly wrens,
rose up from the side of the road,

119

veered across the path of his car,
made a dull *thunk, thunk, thunk*
as bird after bird rolled off the hood,
the windshield . . .

He looked back at the soft mounds of feathers
scattered across the pavement,
the sound still in his ears like the sound
a bullet makes when it hits flesh

He never remembered the sound when he was hit,
only the force spinning him back

And he froze, the first time a friend of his
walked up behind him in a bar
and yelled, "Incoming!"

And he didn't hit the ground
when some neighborhood kids threw a cherry bomb
down the street on a warm hazy night last summer

But he remembered the new guy who stepped on a mine--
the earth and smoke rising into the air--
remembered the way the man's face drained of all color
waiting for the slick that came down too late

When he was a kid he buried
a bird he'd killed with his airgun--
the death ritualized, patterned,
instinctual . . .

Body bags, ponchos--the boots sticking out,
aluminum coffins loaded with forklifts

And he didn't slow down,
the birds in his rear view mirror
getting smaller and smaller, sinking into the pavement
stretched far out behind.

STUDY QUESTIONS

1. Describe the *content* of "A Matter of Fact." What are the
   details? How does this poem illustrate our present human
   condition? What is the *attitude* of the speaker? Does he
   compel us to do anything about what we have seen?

2. How has the poet created two different scenes, and experiences, in "Better Dead than Boring"? How are the two merged into one in the speaker's mind? What are the speaker's attitudes about military life?

3. What keeps your attention while reading "In Northern Ontario"? Does the specific *detail* help you to see, more clearly, this experience? If you have fished, or hunted, try writing your own version of this poem. How can you "show, but not tell"?

4. "44" celebrates the Milwaukee Braves' Hank Aaron. The speaker is eight years old but is the *tone* of the poem developed from an eight year old? How does the poet create visual action? How does the *speaker* feel about Aaron's batting ability? Explain the last sentence.

5. "Winning Hearts and Minds," "Search and Destroy" and "After the War" as well as "Better Dead Than Boring" and "Canoe Trip" explore, quite realistically, the horrors of Vietnam. Look closely at "Winning Hearts and Minds" and try to explore your reactions top it. Shocked? Disturbed? Ask your instructor to bring to class an example of *war poetry* from another era. What are the differences?

Warren
Shibles

The author, a philosophy professor, has written twenty-four books, with eleven publishers (in seven languages) and published sixty articles in professional journals. He is known internationally as one of the leading authorities on metaphor, having published the now authoritative work *Metaphor: An Annotated Bibliography and History* and two other books on the subject. He has also written books or articles on emotion, rational love, humor, reformatory blame, Wittgenstein, ethics, ancient Greek philosophy, death, humanism, poetry, and atheism. His most recent book is *Lying* (1985). He states:

I think there is a close relationship between poetry, philosophy and science. All clarify our concepts and methods of inquiry. Writing stories, articles, and poetry is the most important aesthetic and intellectual thing humans can do. People who begin to write often find they can never and would never wish to leave it, to go back to their previous state. Ideas come which can change our lives and ourselves, give us powerful insight, genuine and honest open inquiry, and produce the highest states of *joie de vivre*. Before these experiences, these creative discoveries, all else falls short. We can hardly say that we have lived.

PRESENCE

At last she has lost
all definition.
She is free.
I do not see her.
"She is standing there."
What could that mean?
Her cheeks are nothing
until they smile
and long fingers empty
until they hold.
Something was there invisible,
inaudible until it spoke.
She cannot be what she
was without reversing time.
She cannot be what she is without
self-destruction.
She is becoming only. We must look
and see, watch. Growth cannot
be seen in an instant.
She is not a snapshot of herself.
A picture of food is not easily digested.
And a rabbit does not hop by
being suspended in mid-air.
To know her is to watch her
and to relate to her
in kindness to
appreciate what is
only known by our
own creations.
I follow her in
amazement to see
what I will
do next.

ON WAKING

The opposite of blue
is truth, of black
the sky.
First the fire, then
the striking of the match.
Racists wash shadows
from the trees.
When in love we smell
the typewriter ribbon.
Female triangles with
a corner pushed in.
Dumb lip noises.
Where all impulses are
the same, the ringing
bell speaks.
Our special animal,
he thinks beyond,
blows a hole in the sky
right through the blue,
is descendant from man
has a female uncle.
And beneath the
circle of the ice cube
sun with one line missing
he drinks his morning ink.

ERWACHEN

Das Gegenteil von Blau
Ist Wahrheit
Von schwarz der Wolkenhimmel.
Erst kommt das Feuer, dann
Das Anzünden des Streichholzes.
Rassisten waschen die Schatten
Der Bäume aus.
Beim Liebesspiel riechen wir
Das Farbband der Schreibmaschine.
Weibliche Dreiecke
Mit einem hineingestoßenen Winkel.
Stumme Lippengeräusche.
Wo alle Gefühle gleich sind
Spricht die Klingende Glocke.
Unser ganz besonderes Tier,
Es denkt jenseits,
Schlägt ein Loch in den Himmel,
Direkt durch das Blaue,
Stammt vom Menschen ab,
Und hat einen weiblichen Onkel.
Und unter dem Kreis
Der Eiswürfelsonne,
Dem eine Linie fehlt,
Trinkt er seine Morgentinte.

ABOUT TO RAIN

About to rain
the wind scrapes
grass grows in clouds
I wait for her
who knows only now,
that morning is morning,
drinks wine, water without water,
to burn and distil the moment;
with whom "sleep at night"
is an aesthetic contradiction.
In the distance her laugh speaks
and eyes take numbers from the clock.
I see the new pine branch
curve up leaving
a half-moon opening
into a sky beyond.
There is something in that absence.
Her thighs shape an
expectant space.
Am I my body or is my body me?
As she speaks, in her voice
there is a space.
We meet,
embrace to close the gap.
She gives what
she does not give,
shares decaffinated thoughts
no cup of flesh
plans against plans
decides nothing.
The dog barks
The involuted moon,
The stars,
The dark clouds,
The usual,
That night
made light with our
passionate abstinence.
Nearly naked
with hair on fire
we fly up
through
stormy trees.

KURZ VOR DEM REGEN

Der Wind kratzt,
Gras wächst in den Wolken.
Ich warte auf sie,
die erst jetzt weiß,
daß morgen Morgen ist,
die Wein trinkt,
Wasser ohne Wasser,
um den Moment zu destillieren, zu verbrennen.
Mit "einem nachts schlafen"
ist ein aesthetischer Widerspruch.
In der Ferne
spricht ihr Lachen
und ihre Augen entfernen Ziffern von der Uhr.
Ich sehe den neuen Tannenzweig
sich biegen,
eine Halbmond-Öffnung lassend
ins Blau hinein.
Da ist etwas in dieser Abwesenheit.
Ihre Schenkel bilden
einen erwartungsvollen Raum.
Bin ich mein Körper oder ist mein Körper ich?
Als sie spricht,
ist in ihrer Stimme ein Loch.
Wir nähern, umarmen uns,
um den Abstand zu schließen.
Sie gibt,
was sie nicht gibt,
teilt koffeinfreie Gedanken,
keine Tasse Fleisch,
Pläne gegen Pläne,
entscheidet nichts.
Der Hunt bellt,
der konkave Mond,
die Sterne,
die dunklen Wolken,
das Übliche,
jene Nacht
Werden durch unsere leidenschaftliche Enthaltsamkeit Licht.
Beinahe nackt,
die Haare entflammt
fliegen wir hinauf
durch stürmische Bäume.

PROGRAMMED MEANING

One word has one meaning.
Two words have two meanings.
One sentence has one meaning.
What is a sum of meanings?
Begin again.
A word has a meaning.
I have a pen.
I have a meaning.
A word has a pen.
Begin again.
A word has no meaning
but stands before us
for an idea
which is in us because
meaning is an idea.
One, two, three, ten ideas?
I lose count.
I become sleepy.
Awake! Begin again.
Hush! Hear the meaning in the words.
Hear it in the whispers.
Press it out into words.
Press grapes into wine.
Pour wine into glasses.
Pour grapes into words.
Pour words into worlds
and if
it makes no sense
do not pour but
begin again.

PROGRAMMIERTE BEDEUTUNG

Ein Wort hat eine Bedeutung.
Zwei Wörter haben zwei Bedeutungen.
Ein Satz hat eine Bedeutung.
Was ist die Summe der Bedeutungen?
Fang' nochmal von vorne an.
Ein Wort hat eine Bedeutung.
Ich habe einen Bleistift.
Ich habe eine Bedeutung.
Ein Wort hat einen Bleistift.
Fang' nochmal von vorne an.
Ein Wort hat keine Bedeutung
Aber steht für einen Gedanken,
Der in uns ist, weil
Bedeutung eine Idee ist.
Eins, zwei, drei, zehn Ideen?
Ich verrechne mich,
Ich werde müde.
Wach' auf! Fang' nochmal an!
Psst! Höre die Bedeutung in den Wörtern.
Höre sie im Flüstern.
Drücke sie in Worten aus.
Presse Trauben zu Wein.
Gieße Wein in Wörter hinein
Und wenn es keinen Sinn hat
Gieße nicht,
Fang' nochmal von vorne an!

QUESTIONS

As a child too young to know I
was an "I"
and still thinking that a dog
chasing its tail
was genuine progress
and that cows have tails
to protect themselves from teachers,
I had a strong desire to
touch a young girl's knuckle
and learn what caused an ant
to walk.
Would one pull on a pigtail
bring down all knowledge?
Why is Eric a mouse and
Humphry an elephant,
and people far away so small?
Do pies have mothers?
How many bugs are there
under a building?
Did questions themselves grow big?
Did I trip my friend
or just move my foot?
Should marriage contracts
include peanut butter?
Was he sewing a plank or cutting a board?
Why do people smile when talking
on the telephone?
I could write a book
of only questions.
What is the right way to write?
And why can anything be bad?
Can weeds be good?
Is religion humor?
What is the difference between
sweating and thinking?
Are works of art ever finished?
Are words accident prone?
Why no one jokes in dreams?
Are numbers things?
And must a
poem have a plot?

132

FRAGEN

Als ein Kind, zu jung zu wissen,
Daß ich ein "ICH" war
Und noch dachte,
Daß ein Hund der
Seinen Schwanz jagt
Echter Fortschritt sei,
Und daß Kühe lange
Schwänze hätten,
Um sich vor Lehrern
Zu schützen;
Da hatte ich eine starke Sehnsucht
Die Knöchel eines jungen Mädchens
Zu erkennen,
Und die Ursache der Bewegung
Einer Ameise zu entdecken.
Würde ein Zug am Zopf
Alles Wissen herunterbringen?
Warum heißt eine Maus "Eric"
Und ein Elefant "Humphry"?
Und warum sind weit entfernte Leute
Ungeheuer klein?
Haben Torten Mütter?
Wie viele Käfer gibt es
Unter einem Gebäude?
Wachsen die Fragen von selber?
Ließ ich meinen Freund stolpern
Oder bewegte ich nur meinen Fuß?
Gehört zur Ehe Erdnußbutter?
Sägte er eine Planke oder
Schnitt er ein Brett?

Warum lächeln die Leute
Während eines Telefongesprächs?
Ich könnte ein Buch
Nur aus Fragen bestehend schreiben.
Welcher ist der richtige Weg zu schreiben?
Warum darf irgendetwas böse sein?
Kann Unkraut gut sein?
Ist Religion Humor?
Was ist der Unterschied
Zwischen denken und schwitzen?
Sind Kunstwerke jemals fertig?
Sind Worte Unglücksraben?

Warum gibt es in Träumen keinen Humor?
Sind Zahlen Dinge?
Und muß ein Gedicht
Eine Handlung haben?

STUDY QUESTIONS

1. "Presence" is an illustrative portrait of a woman. From the *details* offered, what do you know about this woman? A number of *images* show us what she is not. Try writing an *echo poem* where you answer what the woman is.

2. Has poetry ever surprised you? Though "On Waking" presents striking, clear *images*, the poem doesn't make "sense." What qualities of dreaming appear in the poem? How would you organize a poem with a title as this one? Try it!

3. The translations which follow a few of the poems are by Warren Shibles. If you read German, try translating the English poems without looking at the translations. What differences do you see? If you read Spanish, Italian, or your ethnic language, try translating any of the poems in this collection. Show your translation to someone who speaks that same language. This might turn out to be a very interesting experiment.

4. Try to *paraphrase* "About to Rain." It's difficult to do, isn't it? Why is poetry sometimes like this? What does the list of details tell you about how the *speaker* perceives the woman? Does the poem move toward ecstasy?

5. Children ask countless questions, don't they? But Shibles has presented a different "twist" of a child's questions. What is that twist?

Dennis Trudell

I was born in Buffalo, N.Y., 1938. Went to Denison University in Ohio and later the University of Iowa for an M.A. and M.F.A. Have since moved around some and lived for the past 14 years in or near Madison, Wisconsin.

I have taught in several colleges and two prisons; I have also worked as a free-lance editor and in the "Poets-in-the-Schools" programs of Wisconsin and New York.

Since the late 1960's, I have published poems in little magazines and quarterlies, such places as *Georgia Review, TriQuarterly, Ironwood, Minnesota Review, Prairie Schooner*, and *New England Quarterly*. My poems have been collected in several anthologies, including *Quickly Aging Here, New Voices in American Poetry*, and *Ardis Anthology of New American Poetry*. I have published six chapbook collections of poetry, most recently *Imagining a Revolution: Poems About Central America*.

I won a poetry fellowship from the National Endowment for the Arts and a grant from the Wisconsin Arts Board to publish a collection of writing from Waupun prison, *From the Bottom*. I presently have two novels for young adults with an agent and am working on a third.

I write both poems and fiction--both inert, slack, *bad* poems and some that feel more alive during the writing and later. Usually the ones I want to keep and show other people get out of control somewhere in the writing; usually I react to them afterward in some part of me nearer the belly than the skull.

For a long time I wrote poems about my own mind and things near there--my family, my yearnings and inevitable death. Lately I've written more "political" poems, ones expressing something of the distance I feel between the human community we could be in this society, on this earth, and what we are. It seems more important than it once did that my work be of *use*--like a chair or a bowl for water drunk by those making their way down from the hills and missile silos and rulers' lies . . .

I love the way poetry can not only tell the truth but make it dance--the way it can reawaken the splendor we almost forgot was inside us.

THE ART OF POETRY

You can say anything.
That a young marine charging up a sand incline at Saipan
suddenly thought of mittens on a string.
That after hours in the museum
all is quiet; the Rubens in Trafalgar Square,
for example, stay well within their frames.
That the lake of the mind no longer at civil war
must be lovely and quiet, with delightful small fish
nibbling near the surface.
That Rasputin's toenails
must have been clipped by someone:
where are such traces now?
That the impossible sea
is heaving tonight at the flanks
of a ship with lights and music . . .
of many ships, carrying an unguessable number
of indiscretions, and not a few smokers
considering the jump.
That a flagpole doesn't care--
how silly to march past it on a fine Tuesday
in a small group dressed the same
and hitting the left feet at approximately the same instant.
That the air above your sleeping son's head
is as holy as rain.
That nothing is perfect: an unpleasant woman
said on television tonight I should think of my stink.
That the next person you turn to
may be the only one you'll ever have a chance
to love more than yourself.
That a statue is not a fiesta.
That the snow makes so little noise.
That a car goes by. Slows down, stops, backs up.
Pauses, the motor whirring--and drives off.
It is midnight and October in America.
The small towns are left to the leaves.

CENTRAL AMERICAN VILLAGE

The rain that falls on poverty
is a sound saying hearts do not break,
they absorb. After the rain,

the raw sun inside stomachs will brighten the village.
The one above will beckon the hunger,
the headaches: *Come, Grow* . . .
Colors will shriek as they lean their mute boredom,
boredom. Or it will rain all day.
Or an old woman will hear the drumming
on the tin shacks long after it stops,
and then will die. Or a child
will grow weaker and feel like the rain,
the solid piss of it from a drainspout.
And the pig without a reflection,
and the pink sheen that it drinks from
between a shack and a shack--like diluted blood,
like watered wine, like the flesh
of suburban U.S. babies . . .
And the tears of trees around the village . . .
And the eyes hidden from sight in the dawn
where no one walks, where a lone pig changes color
and the road goes in four directions--
and the road goes in four directions like a crude
stick-drawing of a crucifix . . .
And the end of these sentences is in the capital.
No, it is inside the eyes, in the breasts,
in the rain that will fall the next day or the blaze of heat.
The stones alone the road,
between the road and the shacks:
like people huddled together because they are alive and
                                                    conscious,
because their hearts beat louder in a crowd.

A CHECKERED RED AND WHITE SHIRT

I am looking at a picture
of two children lying on a floor
in Central America.
There is blood on the floor,
there is blood on the children.
One is looking toward the other
and seems to see him. I
want to give them to you
and to keep the children.
I want to be worthy of the pale
gold and orange light around

and from their bodies. It
will not happen here or now.

The second one sees nothing,
or very little. And this:
some gauze beside his mouth
is the brightest thing in sight
and seems his final vapor
escaping. His hands are fists.
His left leg is tilted wrong.
There is an adult hand
on his stomach, there is an adult
weight pulling my eyes.
His brother--now I believe
the two are brothers--
has a large navel. He died too,
soon afterward, the caption says.

He died too. The hand went away.
My eyes will go away. Somoza
went away and Duarte will go.
García will go, he will die.
Mexico and Honduras and Lubbock,
Texas . . . I don't know.
If these children's providers
had not been made desperate enough
to fight, the boys would
probably be alive now.
Perhaps lying hungry on an
unsmeared floor. Perhaps
riding in a truck to join
the Guard. Perhaps watching
the arc of a piece of fruit
connect their hands.

This poem will not end,
it will stop. Two boys
on a floor now washed clean.
Or bombed to fragments.
They were born and lived
and then came to this picture.
The one hurrying nowhere else,
the younger one has a shirt
on the other side of his skull
from the gauze. As though
someone put it there as a pillow

he couldn't stay on. Or as though
he had hugged it like a mother
and then stopped hugging.

MADRE, GUATEMALA

She has an Indian name I can't pronounce.
She has three children's names in her blood.
She walked them two days to a village
where soldiers brought a magic truck.

The truck was conjured in the United States.
The truck was returning men who had vanished.
The truck arrived in dust biting the noon
and spilled a clot of husbands and sons.

And spilled eyes in ruined colors of flesh.
And spilled a many-legged creature in ropes.
And emitted soldiers who leveled bayonets
as watchers' mute shrieks climbed the light.

She bruised her eyes on shreds of a face.
She bruised nights for the rest of her life.
She felt her child's hand leave her hand
as if pulled by a father's drawn breath.

A bayonet moved the child into an arc.
A bayonet moved the shine of an officer's teeth.
A bayonet moved above the splash of gas
as the officer's speech widened like blood.

She has an interior face I can't imagine.
She has a child and a child and an urn.
She still stands on that earth like a drum
while twenty men and one child are a torch.

THE ARAWAKS

Columbus sailed the ocean red
after he landed in the New World,
which wasn't new. The blood of those
who met him drowned their gifts

of nakedness, food, water, parrots,
balls of cotton. They were Arawaks.
They knew how to grow corn, how
not to make swords. They made
small gold earrings and Columbus
sailed their ears in Arawak blood.

The New World was old enough
for its people to know that seeds
slowly explode into corn. Columbus
didn't know that. He guessed the world
was round and the small gold earrings
of Arawaks meant rivers of gold.
He was half right. His ships
came and went, and after two years
half of the quarter-million Arawaks
on what we call Haiti were dead.

Here's how they died. They had
no iron, their spears jumped
apart like flesh from Spanish swords.
Or they marched into ships, grew
thinner than death before reaching Spain.
Or died as slaves. Or fell into the sea
of blood on Haiti when found without
a copper token for bringing in blood--
and a blade took away their hands.
Or killed themselves. The Arawaks.

FRAGMENT IN US

A woman lies on her side
between two humans who lie between
two more . . . They press together
because of a chain; they bend
slightly at the waist and knees.

They sway with the ship and ocean
and they sweat. They would glisten
if above them a rectangle of dark
moved and the light touched them.
But it doesn't move; wood groans

and they do. The woman's navel
is hard against the curved spine

141

of a woman from another tribe
who died six hours ago. Spoons:
they are packed like spoons from

Africa to Virginia, and now she
cries out and the scalding black
pins of air pierce harder at her
temples . . . arteries. Her navel
jitters against the corpse, heaves

and the corpse's weight is firm,
is firm. The woman has a name,
but no one breathing the instants
around her knows it. Writhing,
she howls, throbs; she gives birth.

PHOTOGRAPH

I can't believe this one
of the head just to the right
of a shirt that appears *empty*,
drained, in the dirt--bits of dirt
on one-half a sleeve . . . and just now
I noticd the dried, near-clenched hand
where the rest of the sleeve would lead. There's
a shard of bone visible between--
maybe the hand and the head and
whatever under the slack shirt (one button
yet fastened) are still connected.
El Salvador. "Victims of the Mozote
massacre, Morazán, January 1982,"
it says beneath.

                    The trousers are crazy.
This century is an aberration; the German
parliament approved the new missiles yesterday--
And the dead man's trousers seem near-
empty and elongated into most of a circle.
A *circle*, a circle . . . It was unburied,
the corpse; there are other shapes beyond:
a thick gray bone protrudes from something
like a pants leg, through the pants leg; jumbled
shapes and tones; a dark head near dry
foliage . . . a dry dark and dead son's
head. Father's head . . . *Aw*, two rows of teeth

142

around a black absence of scream, two abyss-black
nostrils; and in this detail from the moil
of textures in the background--those teeth,
their upper and lower jaws, are skewed as though
something blunt had caved in the head
or as though the force of the shriek
had dislocated the chin and jaw; it doesn't matter.
Or as though time and dirt had done it.

       It doesn't matter now.
The trousers in the foreground are a stiffened near-zero.
With their slight rise at the groin. And I don't know why
the head is preserved while the shirt is almost flat.
The moments of dirt beside it: dead plants, insect husks,
worn stones--former mountains, fish skeletons, dinosaur
spines, whatever causes dirt . . . they are darkened
from the blood of the head. Perhaps this man
or boy was half-buried. Or buried by the corpses
now spread behind. It's the absence
of chest and stomach and navel,
upper arms and that half of the sleeve and forearm--
of my tears this last hour and crowds
screaming along sidewalks here at the German parliament
and our Congress; it's the *nothing*
from the mouth-shape of the dead trousers,
the wackoid zero they surround,
that keeps holding my gaze.

       And then it slinks
to the stained roundness of the head,
and then it slinks back between the pants leg . . .

39,572
(dead in Vietnam, November 1969)

Thirty-nine thousand
five hundred and seventy-two
times, our way alone, the membrane
between the mind of Christ
and a landslide of lasers and fishhooks
has torn. Thirty-nine
thousand five hundred and seventy-
two pet kittens, goldfish,
have been impaled. The shortstops
keep sliding into second
and out of sight. A scream

nearly four hundred thousand fingers deep
arcs over Pago Pago
and approaches Davenport.

Thirty-nine thousand five
hundred and seventy-two liquid clear
egglike sacs have felt
the explosion of incisors
to no music. That many
fathers, our way alone,
have seen the yawn of chasms
through their pillows (Some do
not know they see).

The navel fuzz
from government issue T-shirts
of thirty-nine
thousand five hundred and seventy-two
young men would smash
plate glass--
"But they don't wear T-shirts . . .
too hot." Some fifteen thousand
paper routes have suddenly disappeared.
The mothers search vainly through hampers
for something to wash.
Tassels have cringed and unraveled
from the rearview mirrors
of a city of cars. An unknown number
of letters now en route
are postscripts.

Perhaps twenty
thousand younger brothers
are afraid of their new sport coats.
Give or take. The nailed man
feels the sting from yet another
bayonet below his nipples;
the nipples have turned to cinder
thirty-nine thousand
five hundred and seventy-three
times. Our way alone.
Their way, fragments of
so many straw toys clot the air.
Their way. . . .
I cannot see beyond
the mountain of eyelids.

NICARAGUA, NICARAGUA

Now their faces are no clear face,
or they are photographs that won't breathe
and word I've said and liked
myself for saying, and said again . . .
the children I saw in Nicaragua
are not here, and I am not the one
I was who saw them there--

and this is not the bed I cried on
after Matagalpa, after Estelí and El Limón,
and this is not the shiver I was
as I wrote in the dark,
bedsheets like a field in moonlight:
"I have never seen such beauty in my life
as the children of Nicaragua."

Now they shine shoes or words
on chalkboard or in books with their eyes,
and their clothes smell and their grins
won't tear and rinse me,
not this morning, not next month . . .
the children I stood near
in Nicaragua move their blood
between the shadows of huge ships,

shriek of U.S. jets planned for Masaya,
for Managua, for Managua--
and I can't return from the lustre
of those eyes; and I can bear
to read newsprint ahead
burying the eyes, but not without
small mouths howling along my pulse . . .

Not without broken sunlight
of the shell-pocked walls they stood against
for my camera in Matagalpa,
the dirt-black doorways,
doorways of barrios: Acahualinca,
Monimbó . . . not without these breaking
my pale blue sky in Wisconsin,

our blue-eyed children's climb
toward dignity and mirth--
our brown-eyed children's lustre . . .
        I will tell you this: green parakeets
come late each morning and fly
into the smoke of the volcanoes
between Managua and Masaya. They are green
and children of Nicaragua
are laughing this morning--

and the parakeets disappear into smoke
and they breathe the volcano,
and then they fly in pairs, in flocks,
back into the light, alive and *alive*.

THE LIGHT IN OUR BODIES

After supper, the children go out to play.
It is a holy truth.
Notice I did not say, "After supper
we go out to play."
We went out to play, as we walked

back and forth to school,
full of the light in our bodies--
which the adult world didn't know
what to do with.
Having lost their own,
they became teachers or irrelevant

to us behind their newspapers.
My parents' love
was as holy as hide-and-seek,
but I couldn't *play* with it.
So I cleaned my plate and ran away,

and came to this place where every night
after supper, the children go outside . . .

MONDAY MORNING

Six painters in white coveralls
and white short-sleeved shirts and white
caps come into a building carrying a ladder.

They march out of step
through the lobby. They try to enter
an elevator, but the ladder is too long.
They saw it in half. They leave the two halves

in the elevator, but each carry a small pile
of sawdust along a third-floor
corridor. This is a hospital; the six men
each speak a different language,
and when they reach a nurse's station
they offer their palms to the young student nurse
sitting there with a textbook. She

smiles and points to an illustration
of a nerve cell. Each of the men gently
pours what he holds onto the page,
and moves away from the counter to form
a short line of men tap-dancing awkwardly
in worn, white-speckled shoes. A woman
in a nearby bed sits upward

from her inert body to kiss death
as the walls around her blaze a new white.

STUDY QUESTIONS

1. A number of Dennis Trudell's poems are based on his involvement with groups opposing U.S. policy in Central America. Using the library, investigate the political situation to Nicaragua and El Salvador. Then begin to explore how those politics are reflected in "Central American Village," "A Checkered Red and White Shirt," "Madre, Guatemala," "Photograph," and "Nicaragua, Nicaragua."

2. Three poems, "Central American Village," "A Checkered Red and White Shirt," and "Photograph" are written in response to photographs. Try to imagine the photographs Trudell has viewed by drawing what you see in the poems. As an experiment in *photographic poetry*, take a photo from a family album, or any photograph you find interesting, and compose a poem of what you see. Compare Trudell's poems to Andrea Musher's *film-poem* of "When the Light is Good."

3. "The Arawaks" and "Fragment in Us" are poems "For A High School Text." How are these poems different from what you have been taught about Columbus and how Blacks originally came to this country?

4. "39,572" is quite different from Dale Ritterbusch's Vietnam poetry and DeWitt Clinton's "Sniper to Point." In a short essay, explore how these three poets present different but yet similar views of Vietnam.

5. What is a vision of death? "Monday Morning" seems in part an expression of how the speaker imagines its arrival in a certain place and time. The last sentence may cue us in to what the poem is about. What are your reactions to this *surrealistic narration* of a commonplace event?

Gerald Weston

An elderly guru who claimed to have not spoken for forty years during the middle of his life (though he wrote countless letters) once told a friend of mine that the only things of consequence in life are paradox and poetry. Some paradoxes lead to pleasurable discussions among friends: life is too important to take seriously; people have to pollute to live; Zeno's paradox (you could look it up). Others are not so comfortable, i.e., living and/or the fear of living both lead to dying, and for many of us to the desperate likelihood of being old, infirm, self-absorbed, sexless.

I write poetry to hold off the future, or at least to prepare my mind for it. With a handful of words I can lean against time. Now there's a feeling. But I also write out of pure ego. I want my poetry to be good, to be available, and to be public. The final pleasure comes from knowing I've written well enough to draw some readers into the feelings that lead me to write in the first place.

Though the subject matter of my poetry varies--love, lust, absurdity, war, loneliness--it is all informed by the slipping away of time, and by the feeling that this is a mean, low-down thing time does to people who have more to do and to experience than they can fit in.

I am an economist by trade. In my fantasies I have often been a ranking jazz pianist. Though the one-wayness of time permeates my poetry I have spent it wantonly through most of my life.

I came to poetry late and awkwardly, unsure of myself, afraid to read my own material to others. Jean Paul Sartre, in one of his earlier writings, suggests that each person's life is shaped by a central attribute or charactieristic; i.e., shyness, boldness, embarrassment, *naivete,* gracefulness. He would have assigned timidity to me. And maybe he would have been right. Yet I read vividly now to anyone who will listen. I'm hooked on poetry.

I've worked a lot of different jobs: gandy dancing, warehousing, pouring cement, pulling lumber in a sawmill, plumbing (a plumber's helper, actually. My birth certificate says my father was a tailor: in fact he pressed clothes in a laundry. What is a story if it's not improved a little?), inspecting crankshafts, doing lab technician work, selling bibles door to door, collecting bills, coding data, promoting cigarettes, designing Latin Squares, working in race relations, teaching, winning elective office, flying military airplanes, and on and on. Besides work there were a couple years of bumming, two wives, and some splendid children.

It all took time.

When I started to write poetry I told myself all these experiences would certainly be useful, yet I have mined almost none of them, and probably never will. However, I am sure they have acted as protection against striking false notes from time to time, and they help make a dense, complex background for whatever a poem is about.

A final indignity is the finiteness of things. Physicists blithely calculate the number of atoms in the universe (without looking it up I remember a number on the order of 2×10^{27}). At the rate of a book a day one could only read about 25,000 in a lifetime. And there are a countable number of trips to the bathroom. It's all stuff for poetry.

SWEET AS ARROWROOT

I conjure women,
naked,
firm as speculation can make them,
perfect to the taste as mangoes,
quick on their feet,
who thrust their shoulders to my lips,
brush my hair with slender fingers,
and sweat lightly as we couple.

Sometimes,
I create a piece of time long enough to change,
a little, the flow of history.

More than once I have stood among musicians.

It never matters. Like the fly
that returns to the very spot I brush it from,
the terror returns.

I mouth a breast sweet as arrowroot
but the taste dries to a hard omen.

I reach for more flesh,
more approbation,
more applause.
The harbingers are everywhere, and multiplying.

WHEREVER I LOOKED YOU WERE

I dreamed you again last night,
bare-legged,
in an ordinary skirt.
All your edges shone, as if back-lighted.

Wherever I looked you were.
An oak tree cradled your head,
its leaves sharp as thistles,
each fold of its bark craggy and large
as the tree itself;

Waves
flashing like scimitars in the cold moonlight stroked your naked
      legs;

Outlined against a stone of polished granite
your breasts seemed fuller than before.

You sat in a folding chair.
Your size was very ordinary,

but the thing is,
you were holding my piano,
its keys precise as silicon chips,
in your lap.
I think you were wearing shoes.

LIKE A GENTLE BREEZE

It starts in the hair on your chest,
is blown by a silent zephyr north and south
imperceptibly,
frightening as an invisible swirling of gnats.

Banks, restaurants and waiting rooms,
houses and cars are all warm.
Sometimes you even complain of the heat.
Still the heat never seems to really hold,
and the cold curls, glacially
toward your head and belly.

> When the continent was new,
> and a gap of climate separated Seminole and Sioux,
> the Sioux knew more of cold.
> Yet the particular cold of dying columbine and roses
> was as chilling in the Cypress swamps
> as on the banks of the Chicapee.

Your look now, even the most tangential glance,
pierces the skin of the present,
peers unbidden beyond.
You could swear the future laughs,
coughs dust of powdery corsages.
Is old.
Is grey.

OUT OF THE BLUE

Four days after the British
bombed Dresden

out of its ancient existence
I am strafing its smoldering streets,
firing tracers
like glittering nails
into the smoking city.

    A witness,
    who might have fallen from a Linen tree when she was
        eight,
    or later wished for saddle shoes,
    swears she saw the sidewalks burning.

When strafing, details are everything.
Feeling cold and warm at once, tight, competent,
I am holding speed,
concentrating on not getting too low--
    (was that a German soldier running,
    suddenly sprawling ass
    over teacup?
    Concentrate, for chrissake!)
I keep on shooting until the street runs out
pull up
turn hard to the right
slice back like a hatchet splitting the sky
and sweep down another street, shooting.
Always shooting.
Until my ton of bullets is gone.

    She says she saw a woman step into the street,
    sink to her ankle-bones in the hot asphalt,
    and burst into flame.

Gaining altitude I can't help grinning.
Right now I would match my P-47 against any plane in the sky.
I marvel at its squared-off wings
and the physics that holds it up.

    Her voice is coming over the radio
    and I stop my car
    to listen to this woman
        (who,
        like me,
        will cool and die)
    talk of burning sidewalks.

THE MECHANIC

I've had some experience with modern tools.
I've shimmed pillow-blocks--in a pinch--by eye.
I've split my freezing knuckles reaching into pools

of greasy winter light to replace a leaking heater hose,
and danced in the snow when the job was done.
I've done delicate jobs, too, as far as that goes,

and showed the kid once that even the hard steel
of a sports-car's brake-line fittings could be mated
while lying on your back in the dirt, by feel.

I've loved the cold metal. But the other day
I broke an unfamiliar bearing housing. A careless mistake.
I didn't see the wedge of a half-moon key that lay

in the shaft and held the assembly tight and true.
I've had some experience with modern tools.

THE PROPER SIGN

Not a New Hampshire autumn
when wild grapes are loot for wasps and sparrows
and fallen leaves cling
to the crisp transparent surface of lakes
edged with granite;

nor the migrating Canada geese,
each riding the other's turbulence,
tracing the flyway's edge
to destinations known to them and hunters.

Not those, but flocks of small birds,
dust colored,
turning in September's narrowing sky--
stretching, collapsing,
leaning north sometimes, sometimes south,
swooping,
sagging into cornfield stubble,
covering all the wires along County P.

In mid-November they find themselves
further south.

154

THE YELLOW BARN

Right there,
at the corner of Howard Road and Highway 59,
is where it stood.

I used to notice, driving west,
how its gambrel roof sagged a little
under the heavy foot of Orion,
early evenings of early April nights.

It was not like most of the dark red barns
that stood on other hills,
and it never looked like it would weather
to the rotting gray
so much admired by passers-by.

I never watched it in storm,
but I saw it, just afterward, once.
It seemed expanded,
as though it had absorbed the lightning and the rain.
It was standing there,
with a peasant's patience,
awaiting Orion's muscular weight again.

FATHER WILLIAM

I will not walk like an old man walks,
slack and fretful,
wary of the pavement and the grass.

Nor will I recall
falling drunk from a lumbering Army truck--
closing my mind to the death of others--
bragging of the taste of women--
and laughing, laughing--

No. Nor will I hate
the Datsun dealership standing
where the angular oaks of Allen's Woods once stood,
or the streets filled with strangers,
or the youth of my children.

And I will not wander like a cold old man
through the fleshless love of the mind,
loving the memory of an odor remembered--

I will not walk like an old man walks.

155

CORNUCOPIA

Knowing that nirvana,
the dream beyond dreaming,
is not possible
because of an untidy act or two;
and knowing further that the button-molder,
parchment-skinned lurker
lover of fog and icy forests
melter of only the cold and unconnecting ones,
doesn't want me--for some of the same reasons;
knowing finally that there is no tax
written or unwritten
on idle speculation

I think I will come back
re-embodied
as a small man,
compact
quick as a waterbug
with an ass firm as a Damson plum
and eyes glittering,

to make love to women bigger than me
fitting between their breasts
like a glowing amulet
curving into their bodies
endlessly.

Or I will come back
as a female monkey of the Macaca genus.
One has been seen
by an observer of these sorts of things
to entertain forty or fifty crowding males
on a sunny Kampuchean afternoon.

A CHRISTMAS

I.

Us kids sat in a corner, out of the way,
sorting buttons and beads from grandma's special jar
by color, then by size.
Except Dianne, already pretty,
who was careful, sometimes, to keep her legs together.
The winter smell of wool was strong.

156

The grownups laughed and drank their whiskey straight,
and each new arrival was cause for another shot.
When everyone was finally there
Uncle Joey, fat and sweating,
pounded a low note on the player piano,
stuck out his belly,
and began his yearly imitation of Chaliapin--
    "Many brave souls are asleep in the deep--"
He didn't hit the notes, but what the hell, he said.
After that we sang Silent Night,
while spastic Tony blinked his stricken eyes.

I chose my chair to face
General Custer shooting at circling Indians,
his fallen horse bleeding from a tear in its flank,
clouds of dust and burnt gunpowder everywhere.
The smell of boiled cabbage
warmed the room
while we each broke off
and ate
a piece of the mysterious cracker
that passed from hand to hand.

Later we played carefully in grandma's bedroom
glancing
once in a while
at the crucified Christ above the bed,
chipped plaster hands bleeding
and face too long to be Polish.

In the basement, where nail kegs were chairs
and a rusty shoemaker's last the lantern stand,
the grownups passed a whiskey bottle and told jokes
as swiftly as cards are dealt,
until Ignatz, who never learned English,
fell down the basement stairs.
Ben and Joey bumped him up again, to his bed,
three steps at a time.

II.

Mother stood in the doorway,
lips tight against her teeth,
rhythmically squeezing her patent leather purse
as we put on our coats.

We were shivering together in the back seat
when she slapped him.
He took her by the shoulders, swearing,
Shook her so hard her glasses flew off.
Broke against the windshield.
Pieces of glass glittered on the dashboard
like the frost outside.
I tried not to listen, heard only some words--
drunk, goddam drunk, I hate your pa, you
sonofabitch if I have to put up with this--
kept telling Jackie be quiet, shush,
be quiet, shush, be quiet--

We all piled out of the car at Uncle Benny's.
My hands and feet were cold.
Frost sparkled in the headlights,
and the maples looked soft as the feathers grandma saved.
Weaving a little--
spewing a storm of winter breath--
he roared to come with me.
Bright with anger
she said don't you dare.
Jackie stood crying, mouth open, without a sound.

> Floating between them--
> between these two people--
> moving without walking,
> I couldn't feel the snow.

> At home
> in our bed
> I held my little brother
> until he fell asleep.

III.

Our stockings were full
and father was sitting there beside the tree,
elbows on his knees.
I could hear his raspy breathing
while we played with our Lincoln Logs.

STUDY QUESTIONS

1. After reading "Sweet as Arrowroot," "Wherever I Looked You Were," and "Cornucopia," try to explore the poet's view of women. What does he celebrate? How can you tell his is a joyful view?

2. Find out about the bombing of Dresden near the end of WWII. Compare the factual information to "Out of the Blue." Why does the *speaker* focus on one figure? How is that more (or less) effective than writing about hundreds of homeless Germans?

3. How has Gerald Weston used the word *not* or *nor* to explain what he sees in "The Proper Sign." What does he see in the "flocks of small birds"? Does this *imagist poem* offer a message?

4. How has the poet brought *animation* to "The Yellow Barn?" How is the constellation Orion used? What is it that holds the *speaker's* attention to this barn?

5. "A Christmas" takes us back to our childhood memories. How old is the *speaker?* How do we know this is a child's version, yet composed by an adult? What words or expressions make it a child's? Scenes like this can easily become *sentimental*. How is Weston's poem *realistic* and *authentic* vs. *sentimental?*